BANGLADESHI
Restaurant Curries

DINE BANGLADESHI

As explained on page 14 of this book, most British curry houses are owned and operated, not by Indians, but by Bangladeshis.

In 1994, The Dine Bangladeshi Campaign was inaugurated in order to make the British public aware of this fact. As the campaign grew in stature, many of the participating restaurants wanted a more tangible connection, so the Guild of Bangladeshi Restaurateurs was formed. Its function is to establish trading benefits and training initiatives in restaurant management and Bangladeshi cuisine, and to promote the Dine Bangladeshi Campaign message with the financial muscle that sponsors such as Texaco, Avon Insurance and the Midland bank can bring to bear.

The Curry Club is proud to be a campaign sponsor, assisting in particular, with spreading the campaign message.

BANGLADESHI
Restaurant Curries

PAT CHAPMAN

PIATKUS

First published in 1996 by
Judy Piatkus (Publishers) Ltd
5 Windmill Street, London W1P 1HF

The moral right of the author has been asserted

*A catalogue record for this book is available
from the British Library*

ISBN 0-7499-1618-4

Designed by Paul Saunders
Photography by Colin Poole
Food for photography prepared by Pat and Dominique Chapman
Illustrations by Paul Saunders
Map by Dick Vine

Typeset by Selwood Systems, Midsomer Norton
Printed and bound in Great Britain by
Butler & Tanner Ltd, Frome and London

Cover photograph shows *Gomangse Bhoona* (slow-fried beef
curry, page 62) with plain basmati rice (page 134)
and *Khatta or Ambal Begum* (sliced aubergine in a
sticky sweet and sour sauce, page 119)

CONTENTS

❖◈❖

ACKNOWLEDGEMENTS

RESEARCHING this book necessitated my first trip to Bangladesh. I am particularly indebted to my good friend Wali Tasar Uddin, MBE JP, owner of Edinburgh's Verandah, Maharaja, Suruchi and Lancers restaurants and Honorary Consul for Bangladesh in Scotland, whose detailed planning and help made the trip such a success.

I am also indebted to Dr A. F. M. Yussuf, Bangladeshi High Commissioner to Britain, who authorised it, and to Mr Jehangir Iman, General Manager of Biman Bangladeshi Airways, who sanctioned the flights.

In Dhaka I am most grateful to chef Albert Gomes at the Sonargaon Hotel and to Abu S. Alam, owner of the Skyroom restaurant, for their time and patient explanations of Bangladeshi food. In Sylhet I am especially indebted to Rasheed Hussain: 'Mr Satellite', and his wife Roosha, who took us here, there and everywhere, and fed us their exquisite food. It was a pleasure to meet their parents, brothers and sisters, sons and daughters, nieces, nephews, aunts and uncles. Thanks to one uncle in particular, Professor Shafique, owner of the Burgan Tea Plantation, whose philosophy was enchanting. And thanks to everyone else in Bangladesh who was so friendly and helpful. Also to Dominique, my wife, who regularly 'long suffers' lengthy flights, the tropics, cockroaches, mosquitos, malaria pills, strange beds and me, but who shares the hard work, enjoys the food and makes my books possible.

Above all I want to thank all the British Bangladeshi restaurant owners and staff whose efforts have made curry so great in Britain.

I dedicate this book to all these people.

FOREWORD

As MY first visit to an Indian restaurant took place when I was just six years old (it was my birthday treat) I guess I can claim to have had a very early association with the British curry restaurant. 'So what?' I hear you say. It's quite common nowadays to see babes in pushchairs wolfing down poppadoms and chutneys, rice and curries as fervently as their parents.

The point is, the year was 1946. There were only three Indian restaurants in London in those days and I was the youngest client the proprietor had ever served. I remember him well, though he and his Gerrard Street restaurant (Shaafi's) have long since passed on, and China Town has taken their places. He was very old (well every adult is when you're six). He wore a long, grey, high-buttoned frock coat, ankle-tight white silk trousers, beetle-black polished shoes and a white Nehru cap. Such dress was uncommon enough to anyone in 1946. For a six-year-old, it was an awe-inspiring sight. The outing became a regular event for years. I got to call him 'uncle', a great privilege, I believe, for us both and he used to take me into the kitchen and give me treats which weren't on the menu. How could I fail to be anything but hooked? Though I have to say that even at that young age, I was no stranger to spicy food. You could say I was weaned on it. My parents were both born in India and we can trace back, to at least the 1770s, ancestors who worked, lived and died there.

I recall the excitement of those outings well. Particularly, I recall how different Shaafi's food was to the curries cooked at home by my granny and mother. In fact, even today, I can still remember how the food tasted. People who go back a few years often tell me that they can remember tastes from long ago, and that those at the early curry restaurants were better than they are today. They may be right – and it may be because in those very early days the food, by and large, was different. It was mainly cooked by Punjabi Pakistanis. Today the curry-house scene is dominated by people whose origins lie 1,200 miles from Pakistan. It is Bangladeshis who form the vast majority of curry restaurant operators. How this came about is a story waiting to be told. And tell it I do, in this book.

But is the food different now from that of my childhood? Is it authentic, or is it invented? Is it better or is it worse?

Madhur Jaffrey, the doyenne of Indian cooking, is on record as saying that the food at nearly all the Indian restaurants in the United Kingdom is detestable. I chose my words carefully there because Ms Jaffrey also hates the word 'curry'. She has told me herself, on more than one occasion, that she feels it demeans Indian cuisine. I have to say I simply cannot agree with her on either count, but I think I know what she means. Certainly the word 'curry' does not appear in any of India's 15 or so languages. It is an English word and as most educated Indians speak perfect English, they not only know what it means, they use the word extensively. I happen to think 'curry' is brilliant. This one word describes the concept of a single dish, or it can mean a whole meal, or it sums up the cuisine of the whole subcontinent. Can you think of another food word that does that? But the fact is that the word is simplistic and, as we'll see in the introduction which follows, it has an enduringly poor image.

As to the food at our restaurants being 'detestable', I am sure this is neither a dig at Bangladesh, nor at Britain. The 'Indian' restaurants in Ms Jaffrey's current home of New York are decidedly worse than Britain's, as they are currently in Europe and Australia. And, for that matter, they are not necessarily any better in India. The fact is that, except for a very few examples, restaurant food is never like 'home cooking', be it French, English, Chinese, Pakistani, Indian or Bangladeshi. The scale of operations and speed of service require different techniques at the restaurant. Professionals simply do not have the necessary time or budget.

It's one good reason for buying a cookbook such as this one, of course. At home you can spend as much as you like on ingredients, take all the time you want, and give the dish all the intimate care it needs in its cooking. The result you'll get should far exceed that of the restaurant. But it will never altogether replace the restaurant. Different though the product may or may not be, it is exciting to go out, glorious to be waited on, sumptuous to eat someone else's cooking and miraculous not to have to clean up afterwards. Hang the expense!

So what are the answers?

I believe today's restaurant curries *are* different and, of course, the food they cook is *not* authentic. But I do not believe they are 'worse' than they used to be years ago. Not at all. They are infinitely *better*. In fact, our curry market is always in a state of expansion, improvement and change. It is an interesting story, and one which I shall tell in the next few pages.

By far and away the most exciting recent development at the curry restaurant is the arrival on the menu of Bangladeshi specialities. These delights will by no means replace or displace all the favourite curries (authentic or not) which we have come to adore. But, for the first time, Bangladeshi cooks are taking the opportunity to cook at least a little of the food of their own country, rather than churn out their interpretation of the food of one not even their own.

So what are the differences?

To answer that question properly, I decided I needed a trip to Bangladesh. I had been to Pakistan four times in my life, and to India 20 times or so. Together it adds up to over two whole years, but those countries are not Bangladesh even though they are similar to it. Despite the fact that there are 7,000 Bangladeshi-owned restaurants in the United Kingdom, and though I have many UK Bangladeshi restaurant friends, I had never been to their country. It was time to go.

Dominique and I went in August ... not the best time of year! We encountered deluging monsoon rains, severe flash floods and crackling electrical storms which lit the night sky arc-white for hours. Cyclone Lois was heading our way from Thailand. The temperature was around 40°C (104°F) and the humidity 95 per cent. That combination turns your dry shirt to wringing wet in seconds once you step out of the cool cossetting of the hotel air conditioning (when it is working in between routine power cuts). Your energy is instantly sapped, and you feel you haven't the will even to walk down the street. As to the streets, we encountered wall-to-wall interminable traffic jams, street riots complete with tear gas in our eyes – yes, it is excruciating – and a two-day general strike called a *hartal* which paralysed the nation. We believed we had seen it all in the seven days we were there! Our Bangladeshi hosts assured us this was just a typical week!

On the plus side we saw some exquisite sights, met some wonderful, friendly, helpful people and encountered, at restaurants and homes, food which cannot be bettered anywhere on the subcontinent. Visiting Bangladesh was a long-time ambition fulfilled. Though brief, it was very rewarding, and a journey well worth making. The trip filled in many gaps in my knowledge. Now, through the recipes in this book, I can bring you the taste of Bangladesh and I can share my experiences with you in the recipe introductions.

On a number of occasions in the last few years, I have been invited to guest chef at curry restaurants where the staff meal has been a purpose-cooked Bangladeshi speciality not on the menu. In each case it was authentic and delicious, and when I asked why it wasn't on the menu I was told 'no demand'. And I got evasive answers as to why they didn't eat their own restaurant food.

I still don't agree with Madhur's 'detestation' of such food, but I firmly believe that Bangladeshi food, cooked by Bangladeshi chefs, has a real chance of being 'authentic' and that it will take off in just the way *tandoori*, *balti*, indeed curry itself has done.

This is the first-ever book to be published which comprehensively covers the food and cooking of Bangladesh. It is a book I have been wanting to write for some time, and I hope I have done the subject justice. And I hope, too, that the strange names of a new language will soon become familiar, and that all these wonderful dishes will become just as much your favourites as they have become mine.

It is fitting that this book celebrates the 50th year of the curry restaurant and the 25th year of Bangladesh. I hope it helps Bangladeshi food on its way.

Pat Chapman
Haslemere

MENUS

THE PEOPLE of Bangladesh eat spicy food three times a day – at breakfast, lunch and dinner. They are great grazers too, and will nibble on 'something tasty' at any other time of day. They are quite happy with the notion of different courses served on plates and eaten with cutlery, which suits the Western diner. Alternatively they enjoy serving a 'rolling course' meal (described in detail on page 21). They also at times serve the complete meal on *thala* trays with bowls. You can serve your meal in any of these fashions. Add as many chutneys and pickles from Chapter 9 as take your fancy. The suggested number of servings are given for each recipe but you can adjust recipe quantities prorata as required.

Breakfast or Tea-Time
—— SERVES 2–4 ——

Tok Dal (Bangladeshi sour lentil soup) *page 52*
Loochis (puris) dusted with sugar *page 144*
Mishti Doi (sweetened yoghurt) *page 156*
Fresh fruit eg: sweet mango and/or banana
Tea (preferably Bangladeshi or Assam)

Light Lunch
—— SERVES 4 ——

Borhani (spicy yoghurt drink) *page 55*
Gusht Tehari (meat fried rice) *page 138*
Choti (sweet mango pickle) *page 154*

Finger Food Buffet
—— SERVES 6–8 ——

Pyaj Vhajia (onion bhajia) *page 50*
Boti Kebabs (meat) *page 74*
Morog Tikka (chicken) *page 80*
Bekti Tandoori (fish) *page 100*
Maach Koftas (fish balls) *page 106*
Begoomi Dolma (stuffed aubergines) *page 125*
Loochi (bread) *page 144*

Anglo-Indian Raj or Mog Style
—— THREE-COURSES, SERVES 4 ——
Alu Chops (mince-filled potato cutlets) *page 42*
✳
Morog Jal Do Peyaja (stir-fry chicken curry) *page 78*
Bagda Chingri Korma (curried king prawns) *page 93*
Kitchuri (spicy rice with lentils) *page 140*
✳
Paesh (spicy rice pudding) *page 157*

Rasheed and Roosha's Lunch
—— SERVE IN ONE COURSE, ENOUGH FOR 4–6 ——
Korola Bhoortha (spicy 'bitter' gourd) *page 112*
Kakrul Bhaji (seeded gourd curry) *page 116*
Lal Shak (red spinach) *page 110*
Gomangse Bhoona (beef curry) *page 62*
Hilsa Maachhi Vhaji Jol (fish and vegetable curry) *page 102*
Atap Chaul (boiled fragranced rice) *page 138*

Valentine's Day
—— A ROMANTIC THREE- COURSE 'CANDLE-LIT' DINNER ——
(Halve recipe quantities for two people)
Pantara (meat-stuffed pancakes) *page 40*
✳
Boro Chingri Korma (lobster curry) *page 108*
Kabuli (chicken and pea rice) *page 135*
✳
Gulab Jamun (golden globes in syrup) *page 160*
✳
Serve with pink champagne, and don't forget the red roses!

Gourmet Four-Course Dinner
Inspired by Dhaka's Sheraton Hotel
—— SERVES 4–6 ——
Shobji Kebabs (vegetable cutlets) *page 40*

*

Tok Dal (Bangladeshi sour lentil soup) *page 52*

*

Savar Pasanda (beaten medallions of beef) *page 70*
Anday Dopeyaja (egg and onion curry) *page 88*
Puishak Chingri (shrimp curry with green leaves) *page 95*
Khatta Begoom or Ambal (sliced aubergine in a sweet sauce) *page 119*
Razma Dal (red kidney bean curry) *page 130*
Siddha Chaul (plain rice) *page 134*
Moghul Parathas (layered crispy bread) *page 146*

*

Patishapta Pitha (crêpes filled with sweet cheese) *page 162*

Curry House Dinner Party
(Some old favourites with 'new' names)
—— ENOUGH FOR 8 ——
Pyaj Vhajia (onion bhajia) *page 50*
Alu Motor Samosas (triangular pastries) *page 46*

*

Morog Tikka Mossala (chicken tikka masala) *page 81*
Peshi Korma (creamy meat curry) *page 65*
Niramish (mixed vegetable curry) *page 120*
Tok Dal (tart tasting lentils) *page 132*
Atap Chaul (fragranced rice) *page 138*
Chupatti (bread) *page 143*

*

Rosgolla (cake-like balls in syrup) *page 159*

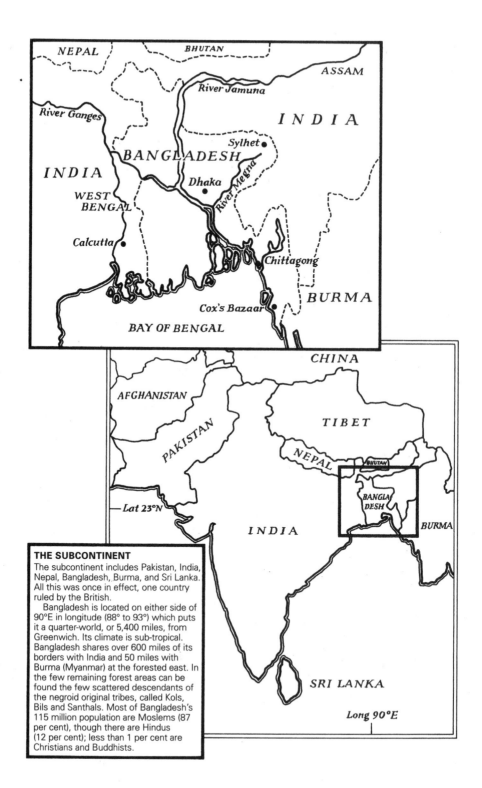

NEPAL   BHUTAN

ASSAM

River Jamuna

INDIA

River Ganges

BANGLADESH

Sylhet

INDIA

Dhaka

River Megna

WEST BENGAL

Calcutta

Chittagong

Cox's Bazaar

BURMA

BAY OF BENGAL

CHINA

AFGHANISTAN

TIBET

PAKISTAN

NEPAL

BHUTAN

Lat 23°N

BANGLA DESH

BURMA

INDIA

SRI LANKA

Long 90°E

THE SUBCONTINENT

The subcontinent includes Pakistan, India, Nepal, Bangladesh, Burma, and Sri Lanka. All this was once in effect, one country ruled by the British.

Bangladesh is located on either side of 90°E in longitude (88° to 93°) which puts it a quarter-world, or 5,400 miles, from Greenwich. Its climate is sub-tropical. Bangladesh shares over 600 miles of its borders with India and 50 miles with Burma (Myanmar) at the forested east. In the few remaining forest areas can be found the few scattered descendants of the negroid original tribes, called Kols, Bils and Santhals. Most of Bangladesh's 115 million population are Moslems (87 per cent), though there are Hindus (12 per cent); less than 1 per cent are Christians and Buddhists.

INTRODUCTION

ANGLADESH is a new country with an ancient curry cooking tradition that traces its roots back more than 2,500 years. For much of that time, as we shall see, it was that part of India known as Bengal. Over the centuries, it became such a Moslem stronghold that eventually Bengal itself became two states with quite separate identities. But before long, one of them became Bangladesh. Her people, her culture, even her language were different – her cuisine unique.

Although the curries and accompaniments of Bangladesh have much in common with those of Bengal, and indeed the whole of India, the spicing is distinctive and subtle. Bangladesh and Bengal use mustard and poppy seeds widely, although their measures and methods may vary. Their important five-spice mixture, *panch phoran* in Bengal, *panch foran* or *porch foron* in Bangladesh, has differences as subtle as those in these spellings. For example, in Calcutta, Bengal's capital, it will include white cummin, fennel, fenugreek, mustard or celery seeds and wild onion seeds. In Dhaka, Bangladesh's capital, celery seeds would not be used, but black cummin and aniseed would replace wild onion and fennel seeds. Bangladeshi *garam masala* will, like as not, contain chilli. Surprisingly perhaps, Bangladeshis adore the chilli and it appears in many forms, in many recipes, not so as to swamp the delicacy of the spicing – rather to punctuate it. Some curries may use as little as three or four spices, and the effect is supreme. Coriander, turmeric and cassia, for example, are all that is needed to produce the Bangladeshi version of that old favourite, *bhoona*, whilst their versions of *korma* are creamy and dreamy and totally mouthwatering. Yet the results are neither tame nor bland. Bangladesh has a unique range of curry cooking techniques such as *charchuri*, *dalna*, *jal*, *kalia*, *khatta*, *niramish*, *rezala*, *shukti* and *tok*, and we'll meet them all later.

I

Nowhere else on the subcontinent has such an array of tastes – sour, bitter, sweet, hot, savoury, mild, pungent and fragrant . . . Bangladeshis adore them all and achieve them by using tamarind and sour fruits, bitter vegetables, molasses, chillies and uniquely subtle blends of spices.

The Bangladeshi repertoire of textures is equally extensive. Crispy fritters and crunchy grilled items take their place alongside watery (but flavourful) soups. Creamy curries contrast with dry stir-fries, fluffy rices with chewy breads. And you will not find vegetables cooked better anywhere. Uniquely, Bangladeshis eat raw and cold curries (*bhoorthas*) and ingredients not used widely in Indian cuisine are the norm in that of Bangladesh. Beef, for example, is the prevalent meat and duck is popular. Tropical fish and exotic vegetables (now available in the United Kingdom) form an indispensable part of the Bangladeshi diet. Sometimes cooked with nothing more than garlic and a sprinkling of whole spice seeds and chilli, these recipes achieve great culinary heights and are ideal for the health-conscious cook.

Modern British curry restaurants, most of which, as we shall see, are Bangladeshi-run, offer their diners a large and comprehensive range of curries, many of which are of Indian origin. In this book therefore there are two types of Bangladeshi cooking. You will find a number of 'restaurant favourites' such as *samosas*, onion *bhajia*, *kebabs*, chicken *tikka* and its popular derivative chicken *tikka masala* curry. Other famous curries include *korma*, *bhoona*, *pasanda*, *jhal frezi*, *biriani* and *pullao*. You'll find all these in the index. You'll also find that some have 'new' Bangladeshi names.

But the greater part of the book is devoted to the other type of Bangladeshi cooking – the authentic dishes that have been made in that country for centuries, and which are just now beginning to find their way into our Bangladeshi restaurants in the West. Be prepared to find these outstanding and exciting 'new' tastes, and some quite unusual ingredients. I have attempted to re-create each taste in its appropriate dish, using authentic ingredients when I know they are available in the West, as well as mentioning substitutes.

I hope this combination of favourite and new will come as a delight and a surprise to curry aficionados.

But before we get cooking, let's put Bangladesh's ancient and colourful history into perspective to enable us to understand not only her authentic food, but the outstanding phenomenon which is the modern curry restaurant.

To do that we must first go back 5,000 years, then swiftly travel through time until we come bang up-to-date.

—— *A LITTLE HISTORY* ——

The first civilised and literate peoples of India had lived in the north-west of the subcontinent in the Indus Valley from as early as 3000 BC. Their civilisation was swept away in 1500 BC with the arrival, through the Khyber Pass, of nomadic Aryan cattle farmers, whose tribes slowly spread across most of the subcontinent, endowing India with Hinduism and a fervent worship of the cow. During this time the lands to the north-east (now Bangladesh) were largely ignored. They were densely forested, criss-crossed by large rivers, prone to annual flooding, subject to almost untenable humidity and inhabited initially by isolated primitive aboriginal tribes. By 500 BC they had become many independent kingdoms, and Buddhism had become the primary religion. The eventual arrival of Aryan Hindus in the area led to continual warring between the rival faiths.

By 325 BC an overall Bengali ruler had established himself, Chandragupta Maurya. It was the time when the Greeks under Alexander the Great had conquered their way into the Indus Valley, and would doubtless have conquered all India had not their troops, facing Maurya's large army mounted on foot, horse and elephant, declared that they had travelled far and long enough from Greece and voted, in true Greek democratic fashion, to return home. Maurya went on to conquer India, thus establishing the first Indian Empire. In size, it was never matched until the Moghuls. Only British India was larger. Although Maurya's empire was relatively short-lived, both Hinduism and Buddhism flourished and grew while it lasted.

During the next 600 to 700 years, although there was considerable warring and change of rulers in Bengal, little altered in the way of culture and civilisation. Bengal was in any case totally isolated from outside invaders by the huge Himalayan mountain ranges to its north and insular China beyond that. India's invaders invariably came through the north-west passage, ousting the inhabitants of that area before reaching inland. Bengal was over 1,200 miles away, and it escaped the attentions of the invaders.

The Arabs

The collapse of the Roman Empire in the fifth century AD created a vacuum which was to be filled by the people of Arabia. The Arab tribes had developed trading routes which linked the various empires across seas and deserts. On land they domesticated the camel and invented the caravan. They learned where precious water supplies were, and how to use and conserve them in their arduous journeys. They invented a reliable and efficient trading boat, the *dhow,* and they learned to use the monsoon winds to cross the Arabian Sea to and from India. They carried slaves, gold, ivory, silk, cotton, dates and spices between East and West, and they created wealth and trade monopolies. It was the rise of Islam which was to unite the warring Arab tribes, and in AD 712, within one century of the birth of Mohammed, they gained their first territorial victory in India, with the capture of Sindh.

The arrival of the Moslem faith in India was to have the most profound effect on the population since the coming of the Aryans 2,000 years before. Over the centuries wave after wave of Moslem invaders came through the Khyber. Bengal in its isolation had been a peaceful haven of Buddhism under various kingships, and it was not until 1199 that it was captured by its first Moslem invader, Mohammed Khilji, a Turkestan sultan who ruled from Delhi. Even though this was 800 miles away, the power of Islam led to the rapid decline of Buddhism in Bengal.

There appears to be no written reference to Bengal prior to the thirteenth century. The much-travelled Venetian explorer Marco Polo almost certainly did not visit the country, but he certainly had anti-Moslem views about it. In 1298 he wrote: 'Bangala is a province located between China and India, populated by wretched idolators, with a peculiar language.'

Another early traveller, Ibn Batuta, himself a Moslem (from Morocco), did visit the country, including Sylhet, and had rather more sympathetic views about it. He wrote in 1345: 'We arrived in the country of Banjala, having seen no country in the world where goods are cheaper than this. But it is muggy, and those who come [there] call it "a hell full of good things".'

Vasco da Gama, the Portuguese navigator who pioneered the sea route from Europe to India also visited Bengal. In his journal, written around 1510, he wrote: 'Bemgala is a kingdom with many Moors and few Christians. In this land are many cotton and silk cloths and much silver. It is 40 days with a fair wind from Calicut [on the Malibar west coast of India].'

Barbosa in 1516 wrote: '... the seaports are inhabited by Moors and Gentiles, amongst whom there is much trade and much shipping to many parts because this sea is a gulf ... at its inner extremity is a very great city called Bengala.' This city was almost certainly the fishing port of Chittagong, or Chatgawn, established by Buddhists over 2,000 years earlier.

Bengal had remained under the control of Delhi until 1338, but its distance and climate, and the fact that much of its communications depended on an intricate and unmapped network of waterways – which the local Turks never troubled to learn – enabled an ambitious nobleman, Ilyas Khan, to capture the area and declare himself king. He named his country Bangladesh, the land (*desh*) of the Bengali people (*Bangla*). Despite attempts by Delhi to regain it, Bangladesh remained independent until it was captured by the Moghuls in 1538.

The Moghuls

The Moghuls were India's final Moslem invaders. Babur led them through the north-west passage and, in a remarkably bold and lucky raid, he captured Delhi in 1526, declaring himself emperor of India. The Moghuls, in less than a century, re-established a culture and a system of law and order which India had lacked since Maurya. As with their predecessors, the Moghuls found themselves a relatively small religious minority in control of a vast Hindu majority. Their strength came in learning to live with the Hindus through toleration rather than persecution. They permitted Hindu Kings – the rajahs – to rule their own kingdoms, albeit under strict Moghul control. By the time of the Emperor Aurangzeb in the late seventeenth century, Bengal was under direct rule and frequently had a Moghul prince of the blood as viceroy. Dhaka, now capital of Bangladesh, became their eastern centre. Aurangzeb must have visited Bangladesh because he is quoted as calling it the 'Paradise of Nations'. It is unlikely that the other Moghul emperors bothered to travel there. Indeed, the fact that they did not do so was their undoing.

If the Moghuls had a failing it was that they did not understand the importance of international trade. They were dynastic empire-builders and warriors, they travelled by land and did not care about foreigners who arrived by sea. They scarcely noticed that the Portuguese, who had arrived in India a few years before them, had quickly ousted the Arabs as sea traders and captured the spice market. As long as they paid taxes to the Moghuls, the emperors were content. However, the religious fanaticism of the Jesuits made the Moghuls uneasy. It did not fit into their lax and debauched interpretation of Islam. They believed that life was to be enjoyed. They drank wine and took drugs, and their sexual exploits involved men and women of any religion. They ate forbidden foods, and regularly broke the obligatory Moslem fasts.

The British

This was the India that Britain discovered in the early 1600s. The Moghuls were more than happy to allow the British to trade with them hoping, correctly as it turned out, that it would weaken the Portuguese. They preferred the way the English interpreted Christianity and within a short while gave them permission to build a trading station at Surat harbour (north of Bombay). The wily British, however, had it in mind to locate their factories in areas outside direct Moghul control. In 1640 they set up in Madras and in 1674, Bombay. They needed Moghul permission for these locations, of course, and this proved to be easily obtained. Both sites were no more than good anchorages at the time. They were not townships. Factories came first, then towns and finally armies to defend them. The officers were at first English and the men largely Hindus, whom the British trained.

It was not long before the British went looking for their next potential deep-water stronghold. They found it in the Bay of Bengal. In his 1688 diary, one Captain Hedges wrote: 'So myself accompanied with Captain

Haddock and the 120 soldiers we carried from hence [aboard ship from Madras] embarked, and about the 20th September arrived at Calcutta.'

Without wasting time, the East India Company succeeded in acquiring the land from the wealthy landowner (*zemindar*), who at first feigned resistance but who, according to diarist Orme, soon succumbed: 'His avaricious disposition, the English plied with presents, until in 1698 they obtained permission to purchase from the zemindar ... the town of Calcutta and its districts extending about 3 miles along the eastern bank of the river.'

Calcutta soon became the East India Company's major port and local Moslem labour was employed in many trades. One of these was shipping and local Bengalis were recruited as sailors, known as *lascars*. By the middle of the eighteenth century, thousands of company ships were regularly sailing between England and India, and their lascar crews were as much at home in London docks as Calcutta.

As the Moghul empire began to decline, the British began to acquire more territory. They already controlled what had been the Portuguese sea routes; now, in a series of battles, they ousted the French and Dutch from India. As they gained more and more land, they were careful to leave nominal control with the local king, unless he opposed them. And they did not interfere with the two main religions: Hinduism (the majority faith) and Islam (the minority one). However, for the first time, Moslems could see that the control over India, that they had enjoyed for a thousand years was slipping from them. For every Indian Moslem there were eight Hindus. Unease led to squabbling and to riots, particularly in the north-west and Bengal areas, the former Moslem strongholds.

By 1756 the Moghul empire had shrunk to Delhi and the north-west. Bengal had become independent under its princely rulers and it was one of these nawabs who, growing envious and apprehensive as Calcutta grew from a swamp to a city under the British, attacked and captured it and, in an incident called 'The Black Hole of Calcutta', caused the death of British residents. The British were incensed. They sent their Madras army, under Robert Clive, to recapture the city and depose the nawab. Clive's success was not without blood, and the religious overtone of a Hindi army fighting Moslems was significant. Calcutta became the British capital of India and, following the total collapse of the Moghuls in Delhi in 1803, the capital of India.

Looked at in retrospect, the nineteenth century was the chrysalis of modern India. To the eyes of the Raj it was a period of tremendous expansion and consolidation. All the accoutrements of modern society were established in India – parliament, the judicial system, clubs, roads, bridges, railways, post and telegraph. It culminated in 1858 with the acquisition of India itself by Britain, and the proclamation of Queen Victoria as empress. India, well used to empire, responded readily to the benefits which ensued. But this was yet another invader, more alien even than the Moslem Arabs of some 1,000 years before. For the Indian population all the old problems were still there – poverty, inequality of the sexes, the age-old lack of control of their own affairs, the Hindu caste system and Moslem rigidity – and, above all, diametric differences between the two religions. The British tried to resolve many of them by undermining the caste system, opening schools and appointing Indians to positions of responsibility, but the seeds of independence were sown. In Bengal, constant rioting and unrest in the name of religion led to the partitioning of the region into East and West Bengal in 1905. East Bengal was given its own British governor and its own capital Dhaka. However, partition was not a satisfactory solution for the masses, and the rioting became so severe that in 1912 the British moved the capital of India from Calcutta to Delhi and de-partitioned Bengal.

Independence

It was, however, only a matter of time before independence must come to India. Had it not been for the Second World War, it might have been in the 1930s. Immediately after the end of the war, negotiations began with the leaders of the Hindu and Moslem populations. No easy solution was to be found and it was with great reluctance that in 1947, two new states were formed. Pakistan was to consist of two territorial zones formed around the strong Moslem majorities – West Pakistan in the north-west and East Pakistan – formerly East Bengal. They were over 1,200 miles apart, and had different languages. The people were different in race. Those of West Pakistan were meat- and wheat-eaters, whilst those of East Pakistan were vegetarians or fish-eaters and rice was their staple diet. Even their way of dressing was different. West Pakistan had considerable resources including the capital city and the treasury of the new state. East Pakistan was totally impoverished. In short, they had nothing in common except Islam. Lord Mountbatten, the last viceroy, predicted that the two Pakistans would separate within 25 years.

In the years that followed, virtually nothing was done to improve the lot of the East Pakistanis and resentment smouldered. The accuracy of Mountbatten's prediction was uncanny.

Bengal to Bangladesh

On 26 March 1971, East Pakistan declared itself independent of West Pakistan. It renamed itself Bangladesh and went to war to achieve its independence. Nine months later, at a cost of over a million lives, and with

India's help, the battle against Pakistan was finally won on 16 November. Bangladesh was declared the world's 139th state.

Bangladesh today is a country with many problems. It is very poor, under-resourced and densely overpopulated. It has severe annual floods followed by droughts. It is politically unstable, has monumental traffic jams and frequent street riots and general strikes. It is hot and humid and has shortages of everything except people. Foreign diplomats today call Bangladesh a 'hardship posting' and airline crews do their best to avoid stop-overs there. Little seems to have changed in the 650 years since Ibu Batuta called it a 'muggy ... hell, full of good things'.

And good things there are. The people are the friendliest and most generous on earth. Outside the cities they live in areas of outstanding beauty and make handicrafts of outstanding quality. Above all, Bangladeshi food is exquisite. The country's recognised exports include jute, tea, textiles and garments, leather and fish/shellfish. They total just $13 billion per annum. Bangladesh has another 'export' ... its labour. The booming Middle East has become a major employer of Bangladeshis in recent years. But there is another, less well-known 'export' in a specific field ... to the United Kingdom curry restaurant. Eighty-five to ninety per cent of all British curry restaurants, until now known as 'Indian' restaurants, are owned and operated by Bangladeshis. Their 1994 gross turnover exceeded £2.5 billion, and that gave them a 10 per cent share of all United Kingdom restaurant-takings.

Much of the profits return to Bangladesh, one way or another. Restaurant owners build fancy houses and although ordinary mortals – the cooks, chefs, pot washers and waiters – may not be able to afford to imitate them (even in Bangladesh land prices are high and building is costly), they do pay regular visits to the families whom their British pay cheques help to support. Measured against Bangladesh's gross national product, the UK Bangladeshi restaurant turnover and popularity is an extraordinary phenomenon.

How did it come about?

THE BRITISH CURRY HOUSE

Although the British ruled India, the actual number of Britons who lived there was never that great. Their stay there was seldom permanent and usually lasted for their working lives of 35 to 40 years, after which they returned to England. With them came a host of memories and a craving for spicy food. The first recipe for curry appears in *The Art of Cookery Made Plain and Easy* by 'A Lady' (Hannah Glasse) in 1747. 'To make a currey [sic] the Indian way' produced nothing more than a stew with pepper and coriander. No mention of curry powder yet but, by 1861, Isabella Beeton's first cookery book contained a recipe which was to establish the wrong method of cooking curry for over a century. It, too, resulted in a stew, thickened with flour, often containing fruit, and 'flavoured' with the dreaded curry powder which, because it was not fried, gave the dish an unpleasant, raw taste. It was a far cry from the fabulous dishes that servants cooked for sahibs and memsahibs in India. Little wonder that curry was regarded by the gentry as being as curious and distasteful as the expatriates themselves.

Indian food might have become more acceptable had it not received a serious blow, one spin-off of which was to give curry a bad reputation that lingers on to this day. The 1857 mutiny forever changed the relationship between British and Indians. And it lost the East India Company its control over India. For over a century before it had been the norm for the Company's officers to cohabit with (though rarely marry) Indian women and to raise families of mixed race. The man, the sahib, became quite Indianised, wearing Indian clothes, becoming fluent in the languages and enjoying Indian food. There was no racial hatred. After the mutiny, the British government took charge and sent a new wave of officers to India. With an in-built disgust of all things native, they swept away any thoughts of inter-racial cohabitation. Anglo-Indians were despised. Called 'half-castes', they were accorded no status whatever in society. Indian food was equally despised by this new generation of snobs. The tables of the Raj became loaded with 'Anglo-French-style' cuisine. Native servants had to learn how to prepare, cook and serve food which was quite alien to them, and totally unsuitable for the Indian climate. Eight- or ten-course meals were the norm, consisting of soups, fish, entrées, roasts hot and cold, stews, game, puddings, and cheese, followed by ice cream, savouries, coffee and sweetmeats. There was not a curry in sight ... and certainly no garlic. Fortunately, curry did not entirely disappear. Once discovered, it was too good to ignore. But it did not appear at any formal meal – or when guests were present.

As time went by, such stringency relaxed and by the turn of the century it was again considered *au fait* to eat curry. 'Franglaise' cuisine had not disappeared for the formal occasion, but a new cuisine, a hybrid interpretation of British and Indian dishes where every dish was spiced, had become popular for family meals. Such cuisine, native or hybrid, was still regarded with suspicion back home in England.

It was not until 1911 that Britain's first Indian restaurant opened in London's Holborn. It was called the Salut-e-Hind but with the bad reputation curry had already achieved, it was little wonder that the venture failed within a few months, proving that London was not yet ready for such weird food. It took a world war for attitudes to change. The Great War wiped out a generation of young men and deflated Britain's morale. The 1924/5 British Empire Exhibition was an exercise in flag-waving. It achieved its objectives in many aspects, and one venture was unexpectedly to lay the foundation for a vast industry to follow. An Anglo-Indian entrepreneur, Edward Palmer, ran an Indian restaurant in the India Pavillion. The operation was so successful that in 1926 he established a restaurant in a permanent home in London's Regent Street. The Veeraswamy has traded from there ever since, making it Britain's oldest surviving Indian restaurant.

Restaurants of any type were virtually unknown in the subcontinent in 1926, and even in Britain they could be afforded only by the wealthy classes. So by offering Indian cuisine Palmer was taking a hefty risk. But, against the odds, the expatriates, the rich, the royal and the fashionable mingled at The Veeraswamy and it soon became an institution. Palmer and his ex-royal Hindu wife, at first using their household Indian cooks, established a menu with a number of carefully selected dishes although, in the ways of the Raj, curry was almost an appendage amongst Anglo-French cuisine. Dishes such as *hors d'oeuvre variés* and cream of celery soup sat alongside such delights as lobster mayonnaise, jugged hare and *coq-au-vin*, with *épinards en brioche*, and *chou-fleurs*. Tucked into all this, the Indophile could find the inevitable mulligatawny soup followed by a 'choice of lobster, game, rabbit and vegetable curry, including mango chutney etc'. It was all followed by 'choice of sweet, cheese and coffee'!

All this, of course, was exactly what the members of the Raj were used to. As we have seen, curry was not served at every meal. But at The Veeraswamy it proved to be very popular, served with great panache by turbanned, costumed Indian waiters. My mother, then a nurse in her early twenties, and not long since departed from the Raj India of her childhood, well remembers her first visit in 1933: 'I missed my curries – all the family did, so a load of us would all pile onto the tube and splash out a week's pay at The Veeraswamy. It was like being transported home to India.' They ignored the Anglo-French food, of course, and it was not until after the Second World War that such dishes were dropped altogether.

Meanwhile the next two Indian restaurants opened – The Taj Mahal in Oxford in 1937, for the delectation of academia, is still there; and the Kohinor in Manchester (1938), which closed recently. The war intervened before the next two opened, both in London. Shafis of Gerrard Street (long since closed) was trading by 1946 and the Punjab in Aldgate (now in Neal Street) by 1947. They had two things in common. They were run by Punjabis, and they dedicated their menus only to Indian cuisine. It was the birth of the curry house.

For the first time Britain got the authentic taste of India. The Punjab is that area in the north-west of the subcontinent which, in 1947, was split down the middle to be shared between Pakistan and India. The significance of this to the British restaurant trade was yet to come. By and large the formula these early pioneers developed was to serve traditional savoury Punjabi dishes such as *keema, aloo gosht, sag paneer, methi murgh, dhals* and breads (*parathas* and *puris*). With these they coupled creamy Moghul dishes such as *kofta, korma, rhogan gosht, pasanda, bhoona* and *do piaza*, along with *pullaos* and *birianis*. Starters included *shami kebabs*, the *samosa* and the *pakora*. Punjabis, like the British, are meat-eaters. So meat and chicken ruled the roost. Vegetables played a minimal role, as they do in the Punjab, and fish was virtually non-existent.

This was the menu. It contained at least 40 dishes and, of course, a technique had to be evolved to enable the cooks to prepare such dishes at the high speed restaurant customers demanded. A system of pre-cooking lightly curried meat and chicken was perfected, along with a huge pot of tasty curry gravy – a golden purée of onion, garlic, tomato and spices – which was prepared fresh every day. Individual curries were 'flash-fried' to order in small, flat, frying pans, with appropriate pinches of spices and flavourings, different for every dish on the menu. The gravy went in next, followed by the main ingredient. Hey presto – anything from a chicken *korma* to a meat *do piaza* could be rustled up in minutes. It was by no means authentic, and much depended on the quality of the gravy, but it worked. Somewhere along the line, heat gradings appeared with mild, medium and hot ratings; and with an increasing demand for hotter curries, the restaurants invented new names to glamorise the simple addition of chilli powder to the basic formula. Madras, *Vindaloo, Tindaloo* and eventually *Phal* curries entered the language.

During the 1950s, copy-cat curry houses began to spring up here and there. By 1960 there were perhaps 300, but they were still hard to find even in large cities like Liverpool, Sheffield, Leeds and Bristol. It was a time when, for example, Birmingham had just a handful of them, Coventry had none, and London had only a few dozen – and even there they were only just reaching out into the suburbs.

Things ethnic were given a boost at around this time with the government policy to encourage immigration from the Indian subcontinent and the West Indies, as a means of boosting Britain's labour force in its first post-war boom. This led to the establishment of a number of new Asian communities in places like Southall, Manchester, Bradford and Glasgow. One community which had been established for decades was that of East Pakistani Moslems in the East End of London. As we saw earlier, the bulk of the East India Company's merchant navy fleet was manned by lascars, sailors from East Bengal. As far back as the eighteenth century some had settled in the dock areas, along with Chinese and African sailors.

Despite Harold Macmillan's 'never-had-it-so-good' boom, Britain's docks were in decline. They were over-manned and riddled with obstructive procedures. Modern handling techniques and European competition soon began to erode traditional ways. Ships became larger, crews smaller. London docks were simply too tortuous to navigate. Their operations soon passed into history. Many lascars found themselves jobless. There was already a severe shortage of trained Punjabis at the increasing number of curry restaurants, despite the influx of immigrants from Pakistan. What was immediately needed was people, some of whom understood the principles of cooking, others – particularly protégé waiters – who had a working knowledge of English. Former lascars, whether they had been cooks or not, flocked forward, willing to learn a new trade.

What they had to learn was to cook and serve Punjabi and Moghul food that was suitable for high-speed restaurant operations. It bore no relation whatever to that of Bengal which, remember, is over 1,200 miles away. That did not matter; by now, it also bore little resemblance to authentic Punjabi/Moghul food. That most of this new wave of staff came from Sylhet, a tiny district in the north-west of East Pakistan, better known for its tea plantations than anything else, was not immediately apparent.

Incidentally, of all the older Bangladeshi restaurateurs that I have asked about the Sylhetti phenomenon, the most engaging explanation was to be found very close to home – in none other than Haslemere's Shahanaz restaurant. Their headwaiter, one Mr Rouf, an avuncular 'old-hand,' riveted me with tales about his lascar ancestors. They had found prosperity working the Calcutta–London ships. Mr Rouf told me that when the time came, his uncles, like many other Sylhettis, made the jump from shipping to curry, as if it was the most natural thing to do. After all, winked Mr Rouf 'all Bangladeshis come from Sylhet!'

The curry house boom continued unabated. By 1970 there were 1,200 curry houses. The supply of lascars was long since exhausted, but with continued official encouragement to enter Britain, it was natural for Bengalis to take advantage of their extended family system. Fathers, sons, uncles, brothers, cousins were sent for and were all co-opted into existing and new businesses. Bengali surnames like Chowdhury, Uddin, Miah and Rahman became familiar and restaurant names began to evolve from the familiar Taj Mahals and Curry Gardens to more appropriate names like Surma, Jamuna and Megna (Bangladeshi rivers), and Gulshan, Motijeel and Sonargaon (Bangladeshi towns).

These earlier curry houses saw no disadvantage in calling themselves 'Indian', even though by the 1970s most were not. After all, Pakistan itself did not exist until 1947 and Bangladesh until 1971. So the name 'Indian' stuck because, if anyone bothered at all, it was probably felt that the average Briton would understand it better. In fact, the average Briton began to take to curry for a number of reasons.

Firstly, there had not been a mass dining-out tradition before the Second

World War. Eating in restaurants was the preserve of 'the toffs'. Secondly, although 'Indian' restaurants were established in affordable, low-rent areas – the back streets – the service they offered had, until then, been unimaginable: pristine clean restaurants, dazzling white table linen, sparkling silver-plated cutlery, luxurious (at the time) red flock wallpaper, candle-light and attentive waiters in dinner jackets. The food exceeded all expectations. The population, until then unused to anything spicy, and to whom garlic was virtually unknown and untried, was totally won over. Even more importantly, the bottom line, the price, was reasonable enough to enable most diners to become regulars.

Thirdly, during the mid-1960s the post-war baby boom was just reaching adulthood, and the trend, which was to continue to the present day, of curry being acceptable to young persons, particularly at weekends, was established. Lastly, television and foreign travel were both widening people's horizons.

The 1970s saw a continued rapid increase in the number of curry houses; and this decade also saw some other developments, one of which would herald a new fashion at the curry house and another which, as yet, would not. The latter was the creation of Bangladesh as an independent nation in 1971. The former was the introduction of the *tandoori* oven. This simple, ancient, clay pot, fired by charcoal, had been invented in the rugged hilly tribal areas of north-western Pakistan, some 1,000 years ago. And there it stayed, until the partition of 1947 caused population upheaval. One Hindu restaurateur decided it was more prudent to move to Delhi complete with his tandoori ovens. It was the first time tandoori cooking had been seen in India. By 1950 The Veeraswamy offered '*tunduri*' chicken on its menu, but it certainly had no *tandoor*. By the late 1960s a new breed of upmarket restaurants was being established in London and major cities, taking the curry restaurant out of the back streets and into the high street. *Tandoors* were imported from India. The food was acknowledged to be sensational and demand for it spread nationwide. Most Bangladeshi curry restaurants had never heard of it and had no idea how to cook it. It did not exist then (and scarcely does now) in Bangladesh. Yet within a few years nearly every curry house had become a tandoori specialist, many changing their name to reflect this. At the time, many possessed neither a *tandoor* nor expertise, yet before too long the process became ubiquitous and standardised. The menu had grown accordingly. Tasty *tikkas* and *tandooris*, *kebabs* and fluffy *naan* breads passed into the curry house formula.

By 1980, there were over 3,000 curry houses. There was a new generation of customers to whom curry was by now part of British life, and a new generation of Sylhetti restaurateurs. Articulate in English, shrewd in concept and opportunist in marketing, figures like Amin Ali captured media attention when he opened a series of upmarket London restaurants including Last Days of the Raj, Lal Quila and The Red Fort. He was not alone, Edinburgh's Wali Udin had done the same with the Verandah. Soon others all around the country copied them. Redecorations saw the demise of red flock, and the arrival of open spaces, wicker and plants, and enclosed, engraved perspex-screened booths. Menus, which by now could exceed 100 dishes, were carefully trimmed back to more manageable proportions, although the methods of cooking had altered little since the early days.

The 1980s saw a new departure on the curry scene: the arrival of very upmarket Indian restaurants. Although not the first, this concept was spear-headed by Kensington's Bombay Brasserie, as an attempt to break away from the curry house formula so despised by purists such as Madhur Jaffrey. The aim was to re-create authentic Indian home dishes, cooked by highly trained Indian chefs. Although this sparked some other entrants into this field, the curry restaurant market remains dominated by Bangladeshis.

A relatively new trend has recently swept through the market. *Balti*, an aromatic, herby, fresh stir-fry, another cooking style originally from Pakistan, was the preserve of a Kashmiri community in east Birmingham for nearly 20 years. Suddenly it became noticed and put on the menus of many a curry house. In a move reminiscent of the growth of tandoori 20 years earlier, restaurant names are being changed and menus altered. Bangladeshi cooks are as unfamiliar with balti as they were initially with tandoori. In time balti will settle down too.

Despite a heavy recession during the early 1990s, between 1980 and 1995, in a trend which shows no sign of stopping, there was an annual increase of around 12 to 15 per cent in both turnover and the number of curry restaurants. In 1995 turnover stood at £2.5 billion and there were 8,000 restaurants, of which over 7,000 were Bangladeshi owned.

But the most significant development at the restaurant is the decision by Bangladeshis to make themselves and their culinary heritage better known. The 'Dine Bangladeshi Campaign' was established in 1994, when a group of prominent restaurateurs decided to promote both Bangladesh and her food to the British public, via their restaurants. Enam Ali, innovative owner–chef of Epsom's Le Raj, Abdur Rouf of St Andrew's New Balaka Bangladeshi restaurant and Aziz Ur Rahman, owner of Oxford's Aziz and Khazana restaurants, were among the instigators. Within months, curry restaurants up and down Britain took up the theme as signboards and menus began to acknowledge Bangladesh. The country's flag, a red globe surrounded by a forest green field, became a more familiar sight. But above all, as the delightful dishes of Bangladesh make their way into curry house repertoires they will become as familiar a component on the menu as the curries, tandooris and baltis which most of us know and love.

With no more ado, therefore, may I introduce you to Bangladeshi food.

CHAPTER 1

※ ◈ ※

BANGLADESHI CURRY WORKSHOP

IT HAS become something of a recent tradition of mine to call the first chapter of my books the 'curry workshop'. That's because, like any workshop, it's where much of the crafting which will bear fruit in the later stages of the product being made, takes place. And, like any workshop, it can be a kind of untidy hotchpotch of important but disconnected items.

In this case it serves as the place to put all sorts of points, most of them unrelated, which you need to know about curry – for example, the equipment needed, cooking processes, special ingredients, herbs and spices. It also includes advice about the keeping of curry, portion sizes, how to serve the meal and, not least, what to drink with it.

The chapter also includes eleven very important basic recipes – ghee, yoghurt, tamarind, tarkas and stock and spice mixtures, most of which can be made in 'bulk' and stored and which will make the subsequent recipes better and quicker.

My suggestion is that you allocate yourself a morning or an afternoon, get into your workshop (the kitchen) and make all you need. Smells, labour and washing up will therefore be minimised to now-and-again occasions, which will be fun to do rather than a chore.

—— EQUIPMENT ——

Bangladeshi cooking has been around in the form of Bengali cooking for many centuries. Unlike in the West, it has remained a time-consuming and dedicated activity. There is no such thing as the ready meal in Bangladesh. Even in the homes of the wealthy and the middle classes, which have electricity (in between daily power cuts), cooking is done the old laborious way by servants who spurn food-mixers and have to be taught what refrigerators are for.

I am not disputing that grinding spices for 30 minutes with the mortar and pestle does not produce the best results, and you are welcome to do it this way; but 30 seconds in an electric mill is, in my view, almost as good and in the remaining $29\frac{1}{2}$ minutes you can cook an entire curry meal. A Bangladeshi cook will think nothing of standing for several hours continuously stirring a pan of milk until it has reduced to a thick liquid. I can assure you that opening a can of evaporated milk is easier and just as effective.

Fortunately for us the Bangladeshi kitchen has few implements that we ourselves would not have. If you don't already have them I do recommend that you purchase at least a couple of woks (or *karahis* – the two-handled version of the wok) about 12 inches (30 cm) and 6–7 inches (15–17.5 cm) in diameter. More than one of each is useful. The *tava* or griddle is a heavy, almost flat, circular, wooden-handled, steel griddle pan used to cook Indian breads, omelettes and pancakes. A large, flat frying pan can be substituted.

Other necessary implements which you will probably already have are:

knives
chopping boards
mixing bowls – large, medium and small
sieves
large, slotted spoon for use in a deep-fryer
deep-fryer
casserole dish(es) – 4–5 pint (2.25–2.75 litres)
saucepans with lids – 6 pint (3.5 litre), 4 pint (2.25 litre), $2\frac{1}{4}$ pint (1.4 litre)
oven trays
grill tray with wire rack
bamboo or metal steamer; an 8 inch (20 cm) or large pan with a perforated inner pan and tight-fitting lid (or a well-fitting sieve over a pan with a lid) can be substituted

Electric Tools

Food processor or blender
The food processor is a fine tool and a good investment providing you plan to use it enough to justify the outlay. It is used in some of the recipes in this book.

Generally, though, I avoid using many attachments – they seem to create so much mess and take up so much space. But if you are familiar with them, you will use them as second nature.

Coffee grinder

An effective way to grind spices. It can handle most spices and grind them reasonably finely. Best results are obtained when the spices are 'roasted' (see page 25) and cooled first and the machine is not loaded past the halfway mark. A damp wipe leaves the machine ready to handle coffee beans without tainting them.

Spice mill

An attachment for 'Chef' units which grinds all spices, raw or roasted, to any degree of fineness you want.

Microwave

A much-maligned kitchen tool, the microwave seems to be regarded by some as the enemy of real cooking. I've heard people say that 'real' restaurants or cooks would not use a microwave. This is rubbish, of course. It gets its poor reputation as the purveyor of soggy pub pies, a role in which it performs at its worst. The microwave is a high-speed cooker with limitations.

Like the food processor, it is invaluable in some roles and useless in others. It is great for fast thawing of frozen foods, for casseroling and for re-heating wet dishes. It boils water fast, is excellent for blanching vegetables and it dry-cooks poppadoms. But in my experience, it does not handle the initial frying (*bargar*) of spices and purées effectively, and it is hopeless for cooking or re-heating pastry.

Microwaves vary in power from 350 watts to 2,000 watts (the latter are ultra-powerful, very fast catering units), the average being 650 watts. Cooking times depend on the power of your particular machine, so your own experience is your best guide.

I have recently done blind taste-tests on microwave re-heated versus hob re-heated curries. It does seem that there is less flavour in those from the microwave than in those from the hob. What the explanation is I do not know. But now I use the hob when I can for re-heating.

—— *MARINATION* ——

The recipes on pages 60, 65, 80 and 84 require the marination process. The longer you marinate meat or poultry the better will be the penetration of the marinade. Storage of raw meat and poultry requires great care. If it has once been frozen and thawed, it will be acceptable to marinate in the fridge for up to 24 hours and no more. If the meat or poultry is fresh and has come straight from the vendor's fridge to your own, providing you stay within the 'use by' date (if applicable) it will be acceptable to marinate up to 60 hours in the fridge. Any marination, even for 24 hours, should be thoroughly inspected and smelt. The meat or poultry should look firm and smell clean.

—— *KEEPING CURRIES* ——

Until recently there was no debate about this in Bangladesh. The food was cooked three times a day and was eaten there and then at the appropriate meal. There were no leftovers – no wastage. This is because the heat and humidity would quickly make the food go off and there were no fridges and freezers. Even now only the middle and upper classes own them. And even now, most prefer not to keep and re-heat food.

For a variety of reasons Westerners think differently. Firstly, we do not have the time or servants to cook elaborate curries every day. Secondly, we can take advantage of economies of scale to make bigger batches. Thirdly, there is a school of thought which still prefers curry to be left for a day or two to 'improve' flavours. Of course, the refrigerator is a useful tool. Given sensible quality control, keeping a fresh curry overnight is safe enough. Provided that the raw ingredients are absolutely fresh not frozen, and are cooked immediately, and provided that the dish is cooled rapidly after cooking, then covered and placed in the fridge at once, it will be safe for up to 48 hours.

As a general rule, any meat or poultry curry can be served immediately after cooking, or a few hours later, or even a day or two later. The taste and texture of the dish will change as marination takes place. This usually means the spices will become blander and the principal ingredient softer, and it's up to you which you prefer. Vegetables, in my opinion, taste better served straight after cooking, but some of these, too, will keep. Lentils improve with keeping after cooking, but rice does not, although you will get away with keeping rice for a day or maybe more. Fresh chutneys should always be served fresh.

Common sense must prevail when keeping any food. If you prefer this method of preparation, I would suggest you observe the following points:

1. Do not keep fish or shellfish curries in this way.

2. If you intend to keep a curry for a day or two, under-cook it slightly, that is, cut back the timings by 10 minutes. You will obtain a better texture when re-heating – simply simmer until ready.

3. Use common sense about which vegetables will keep.

4. Keep the food away from warmth, and preferably in a fridge.

5. Use a cover or cling film.

6. Inspect meat or chicken after 24 hours. Smell it and taste it. It should look firm and good.

7. Heat must be applied relatively quickly (as opposed to slowly) when re-heating. Simmer and stir for at least 10 minutes (especially for meat or poultry) and check that the food is hot right through before serving.

8. Taste during re-heating and if a boost of a little more spices is needed, add them early so that they cook in well.

9. Do not use a dish if you even suspect it may be going off. Forty-eight hours is a long time for any dish to sit around, and freezing is a much safer method of storing.

—— *FREEZING* ——

To the Western householder, the freezer is a mandatory item on the inventory. Like the fridge, it too has its uses and drawbacks.

The main point about home freezing is to preserve seasonal items for use out of season. I like to do this with some things and not with others. I prefer to freeze my own sweetcorn – it tastes so much better than the commercial versions. On the other hand, I think bought frozen peas are in many cases better than home-frozen ones. You can freeze fruit and vegetables raw, exactly as they are when picked or purchased (clean, and discard unwanted matter, first). I often do this, but the textbooks advise that you should cook the subject matter first, or at least blanch it, to remove bacteria and gases. It's up to you.

Freezing comes into its own with the preservation of cooked foods and is ideal for curry bases and sauces, and for some complete dishes. It will change the taste of a curry – it's like a long marination. It will soften meats and vegetables and tends to intensify certain whole aromatic spices, though the overall taste will become blander.

Here are a few common sense freezer observations:

1. Use only fresh ingredients, not items that have come from the freezer.

2. Choose your subject carefully. Some ingredients are not suitable for freezing. Items with a high water content change markedly in structure when they thaw and their texture becomes unpleasant.

Meat and poultry are excellent, as are all lentil dishes. Some vegetables work well – aubergines, peas, beans, carrots and mashed potatoes, for example. Most soft fruit and vegetables and whole potatoes are not as successful.

Fish and seafood work well. Rice is satisfactory but I can never see the point – it takes so little time to make fresh rice (and it has a better taste and texture).

3. Always under-cook a dish destined for the freezer by about 10 minutes to allow for 'tenderising' in the freezing and re-heating process.

4. Take out any large, whole spices before freezing, especially cassia, cardamoms and cloves as they tend to become a bit astringent.

5. Get the dish into the freezer as soon as it is cold. Do not freeze if the food – especially chicken – has been kept warm for a long time or re-heated. There is a risk of bacterial contamination.

6. Be aware that spicy food can 'taint' other foods, so preferably pack in a plastic container with an airtight lid.

7. Label contents with description and date.

8. Use within three months.

9. When re-heating ensure that the dish is thoroughly hot and cooked through.

10. You may find the spicing has gone a little bland, so taste and add more spices as needed.

11. Finally, never, ever freeze, thaw and re-freeze an item.

—— *PORTIONS* ——

Except where stated, most of the recipes in this book serve four people with average appetites. I normally allow $1\frac{1}{2}$ lb (675 g) of the principal ingredient of a main course, after it has been shorn of anything inedible, for four servings. Usually there is about 8 oz (225 g) of extra items in a dish, to give about 8 oz (225 g) per person in total.

For an accompanying main course dish allow 3 oz (75 g) per person, for rice allow 2–3 oz (50–75 g) uncooked weight, for dried lentils 1 oz (25 g).

These quantities are given for guidance only. Appetites vary enormously. One person may eat two or even three times as much as another. Also, the composition of an Indian meal could be one main dish with rice, or a number of main dishes with rice and bread. So, as with all aspects of cooking, common sense should prevail.

If you wish to cook for one person, either scale down the quantities or use the freezer. If you wish to cook for more than four, scale up. Taste and adjust as you go – if you feel a particular dish needs more spices, add some. Flexibility is, as always, the key.

—— THE MEAL ——

Bangladeshis eat spicy food three times a day – morning, noon and night. When I recently mentioned curry for breakfast to a journalist on Britain's best-selling national tabloid he recoiled in horror saying, 'No one could enjoy curry for breakfast – ugh!!' When I pointed out that over a quarter of the world's population (on the Indian subcontinent) did not agree with him (not to mention a further 2 or 3 billion people in the Orient, China and Latin America to whom a meal without some kind of spice is anathema), he did not seem convinced. Another journalist friend of mine, however, swears by cold chicken *tikka* (a leftover from the night before apparently) as his wake-up feast! For those who doubt me, there are certainly some superb dishes in this book which could be enjoyed at breakfast or brunch maybe. On pages xi–xiii I have made some menu suggestions.

Bangladeshis like the concept of courses, so it is the norm to start with a soup or a fritter or *kebab*. The meal will then go on with some curries and rice. It will end with a pudding, usually very sweet indeed, and almost invariably with *paan* (a collection of bitter/sweet edibles, wrapped in the leaf of the betel nut). Paan is an acquired taste but if you want to know more please consult the 'Aprés Curry' chapter in my book *Curry Club 250 Favourite Curries and Accompaniments* (see page ii).

As in the West, lunch is a lighter, quicker meal. In Bangladesh it is often taken at around 3 p.m. or later, and it has some features which differentiate it from dinner. For example, the lunchtime starter will often consist of a *shukti* or *shuktoni* dish (see index) served hot or cold. As this is bitter, a much-adored taste in Bangladesh, it is considered easier to digest at lunch than in the evening. Curiously though, the dishes are often lighter and less spicy at lunchtime than at dinner, which seems to contradict the digestion theory.

Traditionally, the concept of three or four courses was blurred in Bangladesh. In some households the meal would arrive (and still does) dish by dish, in a particular order, allowing the diner to savour each new experience as it arrives. This is common French household practice, of course, except that there each dish, be it a vegetable or a fish or whatever, is eaten on its own as an entity.

In Bangladesh, once the dish is served it stays on the table until the meal ends. This 'rolling course' serving can come as a surprise to the unprepared

Western guest who can easily fill up on early offerings. It is, however, not an unattractive way to enjoy the meal and you may wish to try it sometime.

A typical rolling course meal might be served with a crispy starter first – perhaps an *aloo chop* or a *pakora*. While you are enjoying that, a liquid dish – a soup, perhaps – will arrive. Next will follow rice, which is likely to be plain at lunchtime but flavoured in the evening. If it is a *pullao* or *biriani*, little else is needed. Otherwise, if a lentil dish is being served it will arrive next, accompanied perhaps by vegetables. Meat or chicken would be next or (more commonly) a fish dish. The beloved sweet and sour taste would be the penultimate serving, in the form of a *tok* or *khatta* dish and to round off a *murraba* (sweet pickle) could be served, with poppadoms or breads last of all, not first. The sweet course may or may not arrive as a separate entity. It, too, may consist of a number of different items, possibly including fruit. This is, of course, a description of a rather large meal, but as most Bangladeshi households are rather large (and they have cooks) it works well. Besides, each dish will not be enormous. You may want to try this method at a dinner party – but warn your guests first! Most of us will want a simpler set-up on most occasions, and the menu examples on pages xi–xiii give several!

In days gone by, such a Bengali meal was served to each individual diner on a hand-beaten bell-metal plate, called a *thala* (or *thali* in India), on which was positioned rice, fritters, chutneys and breads. A series of small individual bell-metal bowls (*batis*) would be brought to the table containing soups, *dals* and curried dishes which were arranged outside the thala, for the diner to eat in the order of his or her preference. This is a very pleasing arrangement. Bell-metal is an alloy of copper and tin, easy to beat and shape by hand, whose colour is an attractive pale, silvery gold. For food use, however, the thala needed to be 'silvered' inside and was difficult to clean. Modern chrome or stainless steel *thali* sets, whilst perhaps lacking the soul of their ancestors, are hygienic, and an interesting service option. Each diner needs one thala or thali tray of around 10 inches (25 cm) for the basics; one or two 4 inch (8 cm) bati bowls to hold the main curries; and two or three 3 inch (7.5 cm) smaller batis for subsidiary curries or soups.

Bangladeshi food, like Indian, is designed to be eaten without the need to cut anything up at the table. Cutting is done at the preparation stage. Cooking is designed to make everything soft, of course, to be eaten with the right hand. There is an art and an etiquette to this. In southern India all parts of the fingers are used, whereas in north India it is only the tips. Copious finger-licking is to be avoided, indeed is not necessary for those practised in the art.

Finger bowls can be supplied, particularly for novices, and it is mandatory to wash hands before and after the meal. Those who eat this way greatly prefer fingers to cutlery. Even the most exclusive society is happy using fingers, and it was a recent Persian royal shah who said, 'Eating with a knife and fork is like making love through an interpreter.' Educated Bangladeshis do use cutlery, of course. Though a knife can be laid it is rather superfluous. A fork, and a dessert spoon for really liquid items, are all that is needed.

—— *ALCOHOL AND BEVERAGES* ——

Bangladesh's views on the consumption of alcohol are strict amongst themselves, but tolerant to foreigners. In that, they share the views of at least one Moghul emperor.

In his book *Society and Culture in Mughal* [sic] *India*, published by Agarwala in 1963, P.N. Chopra tells us that various Moghul emperors drank wine and arak. Akbar preferred *bhang* (marijuana), and he enforced alcoholic prohibition in court, but allowed Europeans to drink alcohol because, 'they are born in the element of wine, as fish are produced in that of water . . . and to prohibit them the use of it, is to deprive them of life'. This might be a slight overstatement, but there is no technical reason why curry and wine cannot go together and at long last wine critics have come to that conclusion, after decades of condemning such a marriage.

David Wolfe, celebrated wine journalist and critic, says in the *Curry Club Good Curry Restaurant Guide*: 'Diluted spirits are not to everyone's taste nor are fruit drinks. Soured milk drinks such as *lhassi* are good early in the meal, but too rich for continued drinking. Water is boring, and reacts with some spices to give a metallic twang at the back of the throat. Nor is copious water with rice a good idea. Beer tastes better, but the large volumes can be bloating; and for my palate, beer however good, lacks the depth of flavour to match Indian spices – although it cleans the palate effectively.

'So for me, and many others, wine is ideal – providing it has masses of flavour. A delicate Muscadet or Beaujolais is delicious; even sweeter wines like German Riesling can be refreshing at the right time and place. But wine, even white wine, is not a thirst-quencher. On the contrary, its high alcohol content makes it dehydrating.

'Since white wines generally have less flavour, it must be red to stand up to the spices and herbs. Most wine books say fine wine is spoiled by chillies. But in my own experience, this is not so. The wine and spices do not argue face to face, but slide past each other. As the wine flavour momentarily takes over the palate "forgets" the chillies, then the chillies return and the wine is forgotten. More likely to spoil the taste of wine is an excess of sweet mango chutney.'

I agree with that, although I actually find that raw onion (chutney or garnish) does far more 'damage' to one's palate. However, David has put forward an original and interesting concept. Personally, I enjoy red wine with just about everything, curry included. I particularly enjoy the blackberry tastes of St Emilion and Pauillac or the resonance of a good Australian Shiraz, or the body of Châteauneuf-du-Pape. Spanish and Chilean reds often support curry well and are reasonably priced.

For those who prefer white, the earlier dogma, sweet not dry, has now been challenged by experts like David Wolfe. Gewurztraminer, for example, was frequently advocated as a suitable curry wine, simply because it is described as 'spicy' itself. Really, it is too fruity to hold itself together in the company of, say, a sweet and sour but spicy curry.

In practice these days, drivers find themselves unable to drink more than a token. I have found the perfect solution in the spritzer – a combination of one part dry white wine to three parts sparkling mineral water. Mind you, this in no way substitutes for my favourite curry tipple – champagne, pink or white – preferably vintage!!! Cheers!

—— INGREDIENTS ——

Most of the recipes in this book call for easily obtainable ingredients. A few call for specialist items. Certain Bangladeshi fish, for example, are obviously suited to their particular recipes, and can be obtained in the West. However, Western equivalents are named if you need to substitute.

Some ingredients previously thought to be 'exotic', such as aubergines and okra, are readily available, but a few still need to be sought out from Asian stores.

Spices and ingredients such as ghee, coconut milk, tamarind and lentils are also increasingly available. Often, however, not every store stocks every item. So, if you do have problems obtaining specialist items, they can be ordered from the comfort of your armchair by mail order (see page 165).

Spices

It is the combination of spices which makes the cooking of the subcontinent of India so special. Bangladeshi cooking is no exception. The spices you will need to make these recipes are not too many; neither will they cost you too much. Yet they are crucial to all which follows, so they should be cared for as if they were gold. There are some rules:

Firstly Buy small quantities. Once their packets are opened, the spices deteriorate and eventually lose all their flavour (or essential oils). Use them within 6–12 months of opening for ground spices and 12–18 months for whole spices. Beyond those dates, bin them and buy fresh.

Secondly   Store in an airtight lidded container, in a dry place. Temperature is not important but it is better cooler rather than hotter.

Thirdly   Do not be tempted to display your spices in alluring glass jars. Ultra-violet, and especially direct sunlight, fades the colours and, more importantly, the tastes. Glass is all right so long as the spices are kept in a dark place – a cupboard or pantry.

The spices you need
The list in Appendix 2, page 166, will enable you to make all the dishes in this book; an asterisk indicates that the particular spice is used in only one or two recipes. The Bengali/Bangladeshi words follow in brackets. All these spices are available by mail order. See page 166 for details.

Roasting spices
Some recipes in this book call for roasted whole spices. It is easy to roast them and it's fun and the results you get are stupendous. The analogy is coffee. The 'roasting' process releases those delicious aromatic fragrances, the essential oils, into the air. The simplest way to 'roast' spices is to put them into a pre-heated dry frying pan, *tava*, *karahi* or wok which you put on a medium heat on the stove. Dry stir-fry (no oil or water remember) for 30–60 seconds to release the aromas. Do not let the spices burn, and if you do burn them, bin them – it's cheap enough and quick enough to start again. Cool the spices. You can store them, but it is better to roast them and use them immediately as required.

Grinding spices
Roast them first and cool them. Then grind in a mortar and pestle if you enjoy hard work, or in a coffee grinder, or the spice mill attachment for electric food processors or liquidisers (see page 17).

Factory-ground spices
Many of the recipes call for factory-ground spices. Unlike the home-ground ones above, they are not roasted at the factory before they are ground. So they are raw and their oils must be released, not by roasting them this time, but by frying them (see The Bhoona Process, page 28).

Boiling Spices

As we have seen, the way to 'release' the flavours of spices is to roast or fry them. It is certainly the case with ground spices, and most whole spices.

25

However, there are a few whole spices whose flavours can be released by simmering in liquid (stock or water). These are bay leaves, curry leaves, dried fenugreek leaves, cinnamon stick, cassia bark, cardamom pods (green and brown) and cloves.

Certain aromatic meat or pulse dishes can benefit from this method, and a good example is the Razma recipe on page 130.

Curry Powder and Bottled Tandoori and Curry Pastes

So few of the recipes in this book need ready-made curry powder or paste that I have not included a recipe for either (although all my other curry books have recipes for several types of both – see page ii). Any make of curry powder or paste can be used for those particular recipes.

Oils and Fats

Edible oil and fat can be produced from many vegetables and nuts and from meat, fish, poultry, etc. It can also be produced from milk in the form of butter.

Curry cooking depends very greatly on the use of oil to establish both taste and texture, particularly in the early stages of cooking. And there is no argument that using more oil creates a better curry than using less. There is a limit to this, of course. We are all probably familiar with the curries swimming in oil that are served in some restaurants. In such a case, too much oil was used in the first place and no matter how good the end result, the excess oil will have spoilt the dish. It could so easily have been spooned off at the end of its cooking while still in its saucepan. Once a properly cooked curry is taken off direct heat and allowed to rest, all the oil rises to the top and can be ladled off for future use in curry cooking.

Many suitable oils are available in Britain. For deep-frying I use a good quality odourless corn oil. This will do for all your Indian cookery, but for added interest I also use mustard blend oil which gives a distinctive flavour to the many Bangladeshi dishes (see opposite). It is made from mustard seeds and smells a bit strong until it is cooked, when it becomes quite sweet in flavour. A light oil – sunflower oil, for example or soya oil – is superb for lightly stir-fried vegetable dishes. It is odourless and does not affect delicate and subtle dishes.

These days nutritionists are aware of the health risks concerning certain fats and oils. Solid fats are described as saturated and can lead to a build-up of cholesterol in the body. Saturated fats include rendered animal fat such as dripping and lard. Butter, clarified butter and butter ghee are in this category and, to a lesser extent, so is solid margarine and vegetable ghee. Ghee (pronounced with a hard G as in geese) is widely used in the cooking of Bangladesh and its neighbours, and is clarified butter or margarine. It has a wonderful flavour and really improves recipes like *parathas* or *pullao* rice and some curries. It is expensive to buy in tins, but easy to make (see page 30). Oils described as polyunsaturated are said to be better, and include certain vegetable ones such as sunflower and soya oil. Monounsaturated oils are said to be best of all and include peanut and mustard oils, both of which are excellent for curry cooking. One oil you should never use in any Indian cooking is olive oil. It imparts a strong flavour which does not go at all well with Indian cuisine.

In many dishes the oil will affect the final taste very minimally, so most varieties can be used instead of ghee. But in rice and bread cooking, ghee imparts an important flavour; remember, too, that it minimises burning (see The Bhoona Process, page 28). I have tried to strike a happy balance in these recipes by specifying neither too much nor too little ghee or oil. You can always use more if that is to your taste and remember to spoon off the excess before serving.

Mustard Oil

Mustard seeds are a very popular Bangladeshi spice. They are also used to make mustard oil. It has been used for cooking on the subcontinent for thousands of years and is available, bottled, at specialist stores in the United Kingdom.

Recently, the manufacturers have taken to adding the phrase 'For external use only' to their label. What does this mean? Can it now no longer be used for cooking? Will it poison us if we eat it?

The appearance of this enigmatic phrase is a result of European legislation. Here, from the horse's mouth, KTC Edibles Ltd in the West Midlands, a major producer of mustard oil, is the explanation:

'Pure mustard oil contains over 22% erucic acid. In large doses this can cause allergic reactions and may be carcinogenic. EC regulations stipulate that no food shall contain over 5% erucic acid, consequently KTC carry the statement "for external use only".'

KTC, however, know that this product is widely used in Asian cooking, as it has been for thousands of years. At most, a one-portion recipe requires a teaspoon or two, and you would need several pints a day for it to have any adverse effect. It's like the recent scare about apple juice, where 1 drop of parulin, a natural toxin, per 2,000 pints is said to be above the 'safety limits'. Yet you would need to drink nearly 200 pints a week to exceed the limit.

An alternative to pure mustard oil is a product called blended mustard oil or mustard blend oil. Here pure mustard oil is mixed with vegetable oil, and is therefore already diluted. Its flavour is diluted too, of course.

Mustard oil gives a delicious and particular flavour, but if you have the slightest reservation about using it use another (for example, sesame oil) instead.

—— BANGLADESHI CURRY PROCESSES ——

A number of cooking processes are fundamental to culinary-correct Bangladeshi curries. The most important of these is the bhoona process.

The Bhoona Process

The bhoona (or *bhuna*) is the Bangladeshi term for a process vital to all curry cooking. It is the removal of moisture by cooking in adequate oil or ghee on a gentle, not searing, heat. The process releases the encapsulated essential or volatile oils from whole or ground spices and removes the insidious raw taste prevalent in so many factory-produced, supermarket frozen or chilled curries.

The process is also used to cook garlic and onions (see pages 31 and 32) and even meat curries (see page 62).

The bhoona is detailed in each recipe that uses it. But as it is so important, here are some detailed observations.

1. A round-sided pan such as a karahi or wok is better than a flat pan because it is hot at the base but cooler at the sides, which allows you to control the temperature at which the food is cooking and prevent it burning.

2. Ghee (butter, or vegetable) is better than oil. This is because ghee, being very clarified, reaches a higher temperature before it burns and therefore allows the spices themselves to be taken to a higher temperature before they burn.

3. An initial high temperature is required, but for just a few seconds. The recipes usually average 30 seconds. It could be less. Use your own judgement and remember, even if you take the pan off the heat its contents will continue cooking for a while.

4. The process is used for whole spices (when it is called the *bargar*) or for ground spices (usually factory-ground, hence raw – see page 25), or even for a combination of both.

5. To prevent burning the ground spices, you can add a little water to them

28

(to make a paste) before putting them in the hot ghee. Alternatively, add a little water to the pan just after the spices go in.

6. Either way, be careful of spluttering and stir-fry briskly until the water is fried out (reduced) and the oil separates.

7. Remove the pan from the heat at this point to prevent sticking and burning; the job is done in any case. As the rawness has been removed and cannot be returned, it is acceptable to add a little water to lower the temperature.

8. Once the initial bhoona of spices is finished, further ingredients can be added, for example garlic, ginger and onion (raw). The heat needs to be lowered and the mixture slowly cooked to reduce out all the water in the onions in particular, and convert all the starch (bitter tastes) to sugar. Browning (but not burning) adds to the flavour by caramelising the ingredients.

9. Garlic or onion can be cooked this way on their own (see the tarkas on pages 32 and 33).

10. In recipes where garlic, ginger and onion are used, garlic always goes in first. It is drier than onion but seems to release its flavour best if unaccompanied by either of the other two ingredients. Ginger is then added, but it sticks easily, so watch out for that. Onion goes last. It has a high water content (which you cook out or reduce) which prevents the garlic and ginger from burning.

Ghee

•

GHEE is clarified butter, is very easy to make and gives a distinctive and delicious taste. When cooled and set, it will keep for several months without refrigeration.

If you want to make vegetable ghee, simply use pure vegetable block margarine instead of butter. Factory-produced ghee (usually vegetable) is readily available, but it is never as good as your own easy-to-make version. Ghee, like dripping, becomes more solid the cooler it gets. However, again like dripping, correctly made ghee does not need to be refrigerated. If it does taste rancid this will be because something has been added by accident (on a dirty spoon, for example). This can usually be rectified by re-boiling, skimming and cooling the ghee.

2 lb (900 g) any butter

1. Place the butter blocks whole in a medium-sized non-stick pan. Melt at a very low heat.

2. When completely melted, raise the heat very slightly. The butter must not boil. It must barely simmer. Ensure it does not smoke or burn, but don't stir. Leave to cook for about 1 hour. Some impurities will sink to the bottom and some float on the top. Carefully skim any off the top with a slotted spoon, but don't touch those on the bottom.

3. Turn off the heat and allow the ghee to cool a little. While still warm, strain it through kitchen paper or muslin into an airtight storage jar. When it cools it solidifies, although it is quite soft. It should be a bright pale lemon colour and smell like toffee. If it has burned it will be darker and smell different. Providing it is not too burned it can still be used.

Onion Tarka

·

THE *tarka* is a traditional long, slow fry of thin raw onion slices which become golden brown and crispy. It is often used as a garnish, but is also fundamental to some Bangladeshi dishes when added during cooking, when it gives a magical sweet, yet savoury taste.

It can be frozen and I find it easier (on smells and washing up) to make several batches and freeze them in yoghurt pots. They won't become crispy again, but when they thaw are fine in cooking.

———— **MAKES** enough for I curry ————

8 oz (225 g) onions, peeled
6–8 tablespoons ghee

1. Very finely slice the onions into julienne strips (matchsticks) about $1\frac{1}{2}$ inches (4 cm) in length.

2. Pre-heat the oven to 210°F/100°C/Gas Mark $\frac{1}{4}$.

3. Spread the onion slices on a baking tray and place in the oven for anything between 30 and 45 minutes.

4. They should now be quite dehydrated, so heat the ghee in a large, flat frying pan.

5. Add the onion slices and stir-fry for 10–15 minutes, until they go golden and dark brown. A little blackening is fine, but control things to prevent an all-black situation.

6. When you have the colour you like, strain off the ghee (use it for subsequent cooking). Drain on absorbent paper.

Quick Onion Tarka

•

THIS is almost indistinguishable from the previous recipe, though lacking a little sweetness, and it will save you about $1\frac{1}{2}$ hours. It will keep in an airtight tin for several weeks.

─── MAKES enough for I curry ───

8 tablespoons sunflower oil
6 oz (175 g) dried onion flakes

1. Heat the oil then add the onion flakes.

2. Briskly stir-fry for around 1 minute (they burn easily, so keep them moving). Remove from the heat and drain (save the oil).

Garlic Tarka

•

THIS recipe is a variant of the previous onion tarka. It is for one average batch, but again you can make more than you need (to save smells and washing up) and freeze the extras in an old ice-cube mould dedicated to freezing garlic. When frozen, transfer to double-wrapped bags.

─── MAKES enough for I curry ───

3 garlic cloves
6 tablespoons ghee

1. Thinly slice the garlic crossways.

2. Heat the ghee in a small, flat frying pan. When hot, lower the heat.

3. Add the garlic and stir-fry for 8–10 minutes, until it goes golden brown. It may take less time so take care the garlic doesn't burn.

4. When you have the colour you like, strain off the ghee (use it for subsequent cooking).

Home-made Yoghurt

•

MAKING yoghurt is a skill well worth mastering. Not only does home-made yoghurt cost a fraction of factory versions, but it is fresher and creamier too. To start a yoghurt you need fresh milk (not UHT). You also need a live bacteriological culture called 'bulgaris' to start the process. As this is present in yoghurt itself you can use factory yoghurt as a starter, although this is weaker than proper culture and can result in a thinner yoghurt. This can be thickened (milk powder works well).

Successful yoghurt-making depends on:

• Boiling the milk, which ensures there are no competitive bacteria left alive to vie with the bulgaris in the yoghurt.
• Using fresh culture or yoghurt as the starter.
• Keeping the newly mixed yoghurt warm for the first few hours.
• Stopping fermentation by chilling to prevent it becoming sour.

——— MAKES about 15 fl oz (425 ml) yoghurt ———

1 pint (600 ml) milk (not UHT)
1 tablespoon milk powder (optional)

1 tablespoon bulgaris culture or 4
tablespoons fresh yoghurt

1. Bring the milk to the boil, add the milk powder, then keep it simmering for 2–3 minutes. (Use a 4 pint/2.25 litre pan, and it won't boil over.)

2. Remove from the heat and allow to cool to just above blood temperature, about 20–30 minutes. (It should be no cooler than 104°F/40°C, no hotter than 113°F/45°C.) The age-old test in Bangladesh is rather masochistic and unhygienic – immersing the fingertips in the milk. Once you can keep them in it for 10 seconds it is ready.

3. In a warmed mixing bowl combine the yoghurt culture or yoghurt with a few drops of the warm milk. Mix well. Slowly add the remaining milk.

4. Cover the bowl with cling film then put it in a warm, draught-free place to ferment (an airing cupboard or a pre-warmed switched-off oven).

5. Leave it fermenting undisturbed for at least 6 hours and no more than 8. (The longer it is left the sourer it becomes.) Put it into the fridge (to stop fermentation) for at least 2 hours.

NOTE
Fermentation will stop if the temperature exceeds 130°F/54°C or goes below 100°F/37°C.

Bangladeshi Garam Masala

•

GARAM means 'hot' and *masala*, 'mixture of spices', and garam masala is as familiar to the Indian cook as curry itself. There are as many recipes for it as there are cooks to make it! It is used in Bangladesh, of course, where it is pronounced 'gorom mosholla'.

However, it is not an indigenous Bangladeshi component. It was introduced in the early eighteenth century by the Moghul court (so it's a 'recent' introduction). The Bengali people soon adapted it to their taste, mainly by adding chilli. Garam masala is used in certain dishes which take a long time to cook (for example, meat) to enhance flavours by adding it towards the end of cooking. The delicate aromatics from spices like clove, aniseed and mace are not then lost by over-cooking. It can also be used as a sprinkler on certain dishes, noted in the relevant recipes.

Measures are in metric only because a heaped teaspoon equates roughly to 5 g and a tablespoon to 15 g. The spoon measures are obviously easier and quite acceptable but they are less precise.

——— MAKES about 5½ oz (175 g) ———

50 g (4 tablespoons) coriander seeds
30 g (2 tablespoons) white cummin seeds
20 g (4×2 inch/5 cm) pieces cassia bark
10 g (2 teaspoons) black peppercorns
10 g (2 teaspoons) cloves
10 g (2½ teaspoons) green cardamom pods, crushed

10 g (2 teaspoons) aniseed
10 g (2 pieces) mace
2 g (4–6) bay leaves
at least 10 g (2 teaspoons) chopped dry red chillies
5 g (1 teaspoon) wild onion seeds

Whole Garam Masala

Garam masala can be used whole in a few recipes; use a spoonful or two, as directed.

The actual selection of items will vary from spoonful to spoonful. All part of the fun.

1. Lightly 'roast' everything to release the essential oils (the aroma). Use a dry karahi or wok. Heat it to medium hot. Add the spices in two or three batches. Stir continuously to keep the spices from burning. After a few seconds, they will give off a light steam, but not smoke which means burning – and if it burns – bin it! The steam quickly becomes quite aromatic.

34

2. After about 45 seconds to a minute remove from the heat. Stop the spices cooking by removing them from the pan and allow to cool.

3. Store and use as required.

Ground Garam Masala

Most recipes which use garam masala require it to be ground. You do get an evenness of flavour.

1. Follow steps 1 and 2 from the above recipe for whole garam masala.

2. Use a pestle and mortar if you are a masochist, or a small coffee grinder (Braun's one has good blades for cutting spices) or the Kenwood spice mill attachment (which grinds much finer). Put the whole garam masala cold into the grinder container in small amounts and pulse, then run continuously until ground as thoroughly as the machine will allow.

4. Mix thoroughly and store (see page 25).

Panch Foran

•

THIS is a mixture of five (*panch*) spices used to add aromas to certain Bangladeshi and Bengali dishes, in a manner unique to those dishes.

The spices are usually used whole and fried, but they can also be roasted and even ground, as you will find in my relevant recipes.

I came across a number of variations on my visit to Bangladesh, also some spelling/pronunciation variants. Here are three recipes. Any one can substitute for any other. They each give a slightly different taste, of course, and no one is better than the other. Try them all, over time. You may find a favourite. Make up in suitable batches – say 2 oz (50 g) – and store (see page 25). Experiment also with your own combinations. As with garam masala there are no hard rules.

Panch Foran (One)

This is the version I have used in all my previous curry cookbooks (see page ii). I originally collected the recipe years ago in Calcutta, which is just across the border from Bangladesh in neighbouring Bengal.

The fennel and wild onion seeds give a distinctive aromatic fragrance.

——— MAKES about 2 oz (50 g) ———

2 teaspoons white cummin seeds
2 teaspoons fennel seeds
2 teaspoons fenugreek seeds

2 teaspoons black mustard seeds
2 teaspoons wild onion seeds

Simply mix together and store (see page 25).

NOTE
A common variation is to substitute celery seeds (*radhuni*) for the mustard seeds.

Panch Foran (Two)

This is actually pronounced 'porch fouron' in Sylhet. This version, given to me by master chef Albert Gomes, is distinctive with its black cummin and aniseed. But he let me into one of his secrets. It is the use of a sixth spice. Called *chotaswaz*, it is tiny coriander seeds (to be found in Asian stores with a little hunting). Used minimally, these impart a sweet fragrance to the mixture.

——— MAKES about 2 oz (55 g) ———

2 teaspoons aniseed
2 teaspoons white cummin seeds
2 teaspoons black cummin seeds

2 teaspoons fenugreek seeds
2 teaspoons black mustard seeds
1 teaspoon tiny coriander seeds

Simply mix together and store (see page 25).

Panch Foran (Three)

This version is perhaps the sweetest of the three, with a high concentration of aniseed. Even the mustard seeds seem to become sweeter in this combination.

——— MAKES about 2 oz (50 g) ———

2 teaspoons aniseed
1½ teaspoons white cummin seeds
1 teaspoon black mustard seeds

1 teaspoon black cummin seeds
½ teaspoon fenugreek seeds

Simply mix together and store (see page 25).

Cox's Bazaar Hot Sprinkler

•

IF THIS sounds like a bizarre shower – it isn't. Cox's Bazaar is a seaside town whose claim to fame is the 120-mile beach on which it is located (see page 93). They like it hot there and this whole-spice sprinkler can be used to boost flavours in cooking or literally sprinkled over any dish in this book.

——— MAKES about 2 oz (50 g) ———

5 teaspoons seeds from dry red chillies
3 teaspoons roasted white cummin seeds

1 teaspoon wild onion seeds
1 teaspoon black cummin seeds

Simply mix together and store (see page 25).

Tamarind Purée

•

THE PODS of the tamarind tree encase seeds surrounded by a date-like flesh. The flesh is uniquely sour, a taste as much beloved by Bangladeshis as Indians. The flavour cannot be reproduced by substituting other sour ingredients such as lime/lemon, mango powder or vinegar. So to re-create exactly the correct flavour in those recipes which require tamarind you'll need to make tamarind purée. Unfortunately there is no ready packaged version that I know of and it requires a little work. I recommend that you put it on your 'kitchen-day' list along with such things as tarkas, and freeze the resultant purée in ice-cube moulds. When frozen, transfer to double-wrapped bags.

———— MAKES ample purée ————

11 oz (300 g) block packed tamarind

To use the tamarind block, soak it overnight in twice its volume of hot water – about 23 fl oz (650 ml) per 11 oz (300 g) block. The next day pulp it well with your fingers, then strain through a sieve, discarding the husks and seeds. The brown liquid should be quite thick, and there will be plenty.

Akhni Stock

•

SOMETIMES called *yakhni*, this is a strained clear liquid which is easy to make and can be used like vegetable stock or any time a recipe directs 'add water'. You can keep it in the fridge for a couple of days, but it is essential to re-boil it after this time; it will be safe for several re-boils.

———— MAKES 1½ pints (900 ml) ————

1 lb (450 g) onions, chopped	**SPICES (WHOLE)**
4–6 garlic cloves, chopped	10 cloves
2 inch (5 cm) piece fresh ginger, chopped	10 green cardamom pods
1 tablespoon ghee	6 pieces cassia bark
2 teaspoons salt	6 bay leaves

1. Boil 3 pints (1.75 litres) water, then add everything else.

2. Simmer for 1 hour with the lid on, by which time the stock should have reduced by half. Strain and discard the solids.

CHAPTER 2

─────── ⤜◈⤛ ───────

STARTERS

 $\quad$ WE SAW on page 21, that Bangladeshis enjoy eating their meals in courses, so starters are as popular there as over here.

In this chapter are grouped a carefully selected choice of items ranging from rissoles and fritters, through stuffed pastries (*samosas* and *shingaras*) and pancakes to soups and savoury beverages. These can be regarded as 'any time' snacks or starters. Other recipes in the book can also be used for these purposes, for example the meat *kebabs* on pages 57, 61 and 74 and chicken *pakora* and *tikka* from pages 79 and 80, the prawns on pages 91 and 92 and the *bekti* (fish) tandoori on page 100. From the vegetable chapter there are dishes such as *korola shukto* (page 114), spicy 'bitter' gourd (page 112), fried sliced *kakrul* (page 115), the aubergine *pakoras* (page 118) and the stuffed items (*dolmas*) on pages 125 and 126.

In addition the cold *bhoorthas* (purées) from Chapter 9 (page 149) can always accompany any of the dishes mentioned in, and from, this chapter.

Shobji Kebabs

VEGETABLE CUTLETS

•

I CAME across this delightful vegetable cutlet at the pretty Bithika restaurant at the Dhaka Sheraton Hotel. They were served with this simple sauce and Bangladeshi Garnish (see page 150).

——— MAKES 4 cutlets ———

2 teaspoons mustard blend oil
1 garlic clove, finely chopped
4 tablespoons vegetable oil

MIXTURE
12 oz (350 g) finely mashed potato
4 oz (110 g) cooked carrot, very finely
    chopped
4 oz (110 g) cooked peas, mashed
2 teaspoons cornflour
1 tablespoon finely chopped fresh coriander
    leaves
1 tablespoon finely chopped chives
$\frac{1}{2}$ teaspoon finely chopped fresh basil leaves
1–2 green cayenne chillies, chopped
1 teaspoon minced garlic
$\frac{1}{2}$ teaspoon salt

SPICES
$\frac{2}{3}$ teaspoon ground coriander
$\frac{1}{2}$ teaspoon black mustard seeds
$\frac{1}{3}$ teaspoon turmeric

COATING
3 oz (75 g) breadcrumbs
1 teaspoon Bangladeshi Garam Masala (see
    page 34)
2 eggs, beaten

SAUCE (OPTIONAL)
1 tablespoon ghee
1 teaspoon turmeric
3 teaspoons ground coriander
1 green chilli, finely chopped (optional)
4 tablespoons very finely chopped fresh
    coriander leaves
salt to taste

THE CUTLETS

1. Heat the mustard oil and stir-fry the garlic for about 30 seconds ensuring it does not go brown. Add the **spices** and a splash or two of water and fry for about 30 seconds more.

2. Put the mixture ingredients into a large bowl. Add the fried ingredients and combine thoroughly to create a mouldable mixture. Sometimes this can be a bit dry, so add splashes of water if needed.

3. Divide the mixture into four equal-sized portions and mould them into flat bay leaf shapes, about $\frac{3}{4}$ inch (2 cm) thick.

4. Mix the breadcrumbs and garam masala on a board and put the eggs into a saucer. Dip each cutlet in egg, then dab it around in the breadcrumbs until evenly coated.

5. Heat the vegetable oil in a large, flat frying pan. Fry the cutlets on one side until brown, then turn over and repeat for the other side (allow about 3–5 minutes per side).

THE SAUCE (optional)

1. Heat the ghee, add the turmeric, ground coriander, chilli and chopped coriander leaves. Briskly stir-fry, adding just enough water, little by little, to prevent sticking. After a minute, remove from the heat, add salt to taste and transfer to a serving dish. The sauce can be served hot or cold.

Alu Chops
MINCE-FILLED POTATO CUTLETS
•

THIS was my granny's favourite. She learnt it in her time in the Raj. It is a little time-consuming to make if you start from scratch. But I suggest you make a large batch (double or quadruple the quantities given) and freeze them for later. Mind you, they are so delicious they may never reach the freezer! Serve with the sauce from the previous recipe (page 41) and Bangladeshi Garnish (see page 150).

——— MAKES 4 large chops or 8 small ones ———

MINCE (KEEMA)
2 tablespoons ghee
2 garlic cloves, finely chopped
2 oz (50 g) onion, finely chopped
6 oz (175 g) finely minced lean beef
1–2 green cayenne chillies, finely chopped
1 tablespoon finely chopped fresh coriander leaves
1 teaspoon salt

SPICES
$\frac{1}{2}$ teaspoon turmeric
2 teaspoons ground coriander

$\frac{1}{3}$ teaspoon coriander seeds, crushed
a pinch of wild onion seeds
$\frac{1}{4}$ teaspoon ground cloves

COATING
3 oz (75 g) breadcrumbs
1 teaspoon Bangladeshi Garam Masala (see page 38)
2 eggs, beaten
12 oz (350 g) finely mashed potato
4 tablespoons vegetable oil

THE MINCE

1. Heat the ghee in a karahi or wok. Stir-fry the garlic for 30 seconds. Add the **spices** and stir-fry for 30 seconds then add a tiny amount of water, enough to loosen the mixture, and continue to stir-fry for 30 seconds more.

2. Add the onion and stir-fry, on a lower heat, for about 5 minutes.

3. Add the mince, chillies, chopped coriander leaves and salt and stir-fry at a low simmer for about half-an-hour. Add splashes of water when needed.

4. Allow to cool then divide it into four or eight.

THE CUTLETS

1. Ensure the potato is finely mashed and lump-free. Divide it into four or eight.

2. Make a 'cup' shape of one lump. Put one of the mince quarters or eighths into the cup. Carefully close the cup, so that the mince is encased.

3. Mix the breadcrumbs and garam masala on a board and put the eggs into a saucer. Dip each cutlet in egg, then dab it around in the breadcrumbs until evenly coated.

4. Heat the vegetable oil in a large, flat frying pan. Fry the cutlets on one side until brown, then turn over and repeat for the other side (allow about 3–5 minutes per side).

—— *Variation* ——

Shobji chop For really exotic, delicious cutlets, use slightly more than half of the vegetable cutlet recipe (page 40, prepared to the end of stage 2 of that recipe) instead of mashed potato to encase the mince.

Pantara

MINCE MEAT (KEEMA) STUFFED PANCAKES

•

A DELIGHTFUL starter, unique to Bangladesh. The pancake is made first then it is folded over the cooked, curried mince keema. The whole item is egg-breadcrumbed and pan-fried. Serve it hot or cold with Bangladeshi Garnish (see page 150) and chutneys.

——— MAKES 4 pantara ———

MINCE (KEEMA)
2 tablespoons ghee
2 garlic cloves, finely chopped
2 oz (50 g) onion, finely chopped
6 oz (175 g) finely minced lean beef
1–2 green cayenne chillies, finely chopped
1 tablespoon finely chopped fresh coriander
  leaves
1 teaspoon salt

SPICES
$\frac{1}{2}$ teaspoon turmeric
2 teaspoons ground coriander
$\frac{1}{3}$ teaspoon coriander seeds, crushed

a pinch of wild onion seeds
$\frac{1}{4}$ teaspoon ground cloves

PANCAKES
5 fl oz (150 ml) milk
2 eggs
1 tablespoon sunflower oil
2 oz (50 g) plain white flour
4 teaspoons butter ghee

COATING
3 oz (75 g) breadcrumbs
1 teaspoon Bangladeshi Garam Masala (see page 34)
2 eggs, beaten
2 tablespoons vegetable oil

THE MINCE
Follow the recipe on page 42. Allow it to cool then divide it into four.

THE PANCAKES
These are cooked next. They can be allowed to cool if you wish and can be stored by interleaving each one with kitchen foil or greaseproof paper if they go in the fridge.

1. Measure the milk into a measuring jug. Break the eggs into it. Add the oil. Whisk with a fork.

2. Sift the flour into a large bowl. Slowly pour the milk and egg mixture into the flour, whisking carefully as you go, avoiding lumps.

3. In a very hot tava or omelette pan heat 1 teaspoon of ghee. Pour in a quarter of the batter which, when 'swilled' around the pan, makes a thin pancake. Once it sets turn it over carefully and a few seconds later remove it from the pan.

4. Repeat with the other three pancakes.

FINISHING OFF

1. Mix the breadcrumbs and garam masala on a board and put the eggs into a saucer.

2. When the pancakes are cool enough to handle, spread a quarter of the keema on one-third of one of the pancakes.

3. Roll up the pancake.

4. Dip it in the egg, then roll it in the breadcrumbs.

5. Using a little vegetable oil, fry the pancake in the tava or omelette pan until golden, turning as needed.

6. Repeat with the other three pancakes.

Alu Motor Samosas

TRIANGULAR PASTRIES STUFFED WITH POTATO AND PEAS

•

THERE can be no one in the United Kingdom who doesn't know and love the *samosa*. It's the same in Bangladesh. Street stalls, shack cafés, food shops and high-class restaurants – they all sell them. The pastry should be crackling crisp (here we achieve this with readily available Chinese pastry). The filling should be rewardingly spicy. Here it is the all-traditional *alu* (mashed potato) and *motor* (peas) stuffing. Serve with Bangladeshi Garnish (see page 150) and chutneys.

Make a double or treble batch and freeze the samosas after cooking. Reheat them in the oven (not the microwave) to get them crackling again.

CHEF'S TIP

Some Asian stores sell packets of 'samosa pads' containing about 40 sheets of thinly rolled pastry strips.

——— MAKES 16 samosas ———

FILLING

1 lb (450 g) mashed potato
8 oz (225 g) cooked peas
2 tablespoons finely chopped fresh coriander leaves
1–2 fresh green chillies, chopped
1 teaspoon roasted white cummin seeds
1 teaspoon Bangladeshi Garam Masala (see page 38)
1 teaspoon salt

PASTE

flour and water

PASTRY

16 rectangular sheets of Chinese spring roll pastry or filo pastry, cut to approximately 3 × 8 inches (7.5 × 20 cm)

oil for deep-frying

1. Make the filling first. Allow it sufficient time to cool, then mix all the ingredients together.

2. Mix the flour and water to get a suitable paste.

3. Have a clean, damp tea towel ready. Open the Chinese spring roll pastry packet and pull out enough sheets to create 16 or so rectangles (see note). Cover them with the tea towel to keep them from drying up and going brittle.

4. Take one rectangle. Place a teaspoon of filling on it (see diagram). Make the first diagonal fold, then the second and third.

5. Open the pouch and top up with some more filling. Do not overfill, or it will burst when cooked.

6. Brush some flour and water paste on the next triangle and fold the filled pouch over it to seal in the filling. Trim off the excess.

7. Deep-fry in hot oil at 375°F/190°C for 8–10 minutes.

NOTE
You can get more samosas from this filling. Simply cut more rectangles, and use less filling per samosa.

——— *Variations* ———

Shobji samosa (vegetable filling) and **Keema samosa** (mince filling). Simply use either of the fillings detailed on pages 40 and 42.

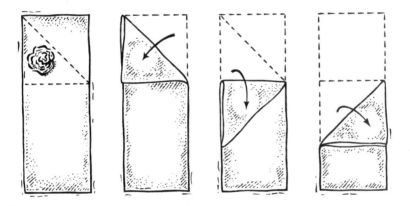

Shingara

CONICAL STUFFED PASTRIES

•

THINK of the Bangladeshi *shingara* as conical *samosas* made from soft short-crust pastry. No triangular lines here. They sit like little dumpy sacks. Fillings can be vegetable, pea and potato or minced meat. And that's convenient because we've done recipes for these already on pages 40, 42 and 46. Serve with Bangladeshi Garnish (see page 150) and chutneys.

Make a double or treble batch of shingaras and freeze them after cooking. Re-heat in the oven (not the microwave) to get them crackling again.

——— MAKES 8 shingara ———

PASTRY

8 oz (225 g) strong white plain flour, plus a little for sprinkling (optional)

½ teaspoon salt

1 teaspoon Bangladeshi Garam Masala (see page 34)

1 tablespoon mustard blend oil

PASTE

flour and water

FILLINGS

About 8 oz (225 g) Shobji Kebab mixture (see page 40) or all the Keema mixture (see page 42) or 8 oz (225 g) Alu Motor mixture (see page 46)

ghee for glazing or oil for deep-frying

1. Make the pastry first. Sieve the flour into a large bowl. Add the salt and garam masala, and mix in. Add the oil and enough water little by little, kneading the dough until it leaves the sides of the bowl clean. (For more dough tips, see page 142). Stand for at least 1 hour.

2. Make a flour and water paste in a bowl (to glue the shingaras together).

3. Have your chosen filling(s) standing by.

4. Divide the dough into four equal parts and roll them into balls. Roll out the balls (you may need a little flour to sprinkle) into discs about 8 inches (20 cm) in diameter.

5. Cut the discs in half.

6. Place one half-disc on a work surface (diagram a). Fold over one-third (b). Paste the top third with the flour and water paste. Then fold over the next third on top (c). You now have an open cone (d.).

7. Spoon a dollop of filling into the cone (not too much or it will burst when frying), then fold over the top, sealing securely and liberally with paste.

48

8. Repeat with the remaining seven discs.

9. The shingara can be oven baked (glaze first with ghee) at 375°F/190°C/Gas Mark 5 for 12–15 minutes or they can be deep-fried at the same temperature for the same time.

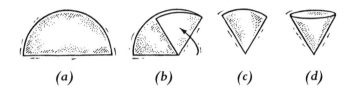

(a)   *(b)*   *(c)*   *(d)*

Pyaj Vhaja
ONION BHAJIA (FRITTERS)

•

HERE is an old friend with a totally new name. *Pyaj* or *peyaja* means 'onion' in Bangladeshi and *vhaja* (or *bhaja*) means 'fried' so it's the age-old fritter so popular at the curry house. It is equally popular in Bangladesh. This recipe is from my *Curry Club Indian Vegetarian Cookbook* (see page ii). No apologies for that – it's a really well-tested well-tried recipe – one which I often use when I do my appearances at shows and exhibitions so I know it has been enjoyed by thousands.

Serve with Bangladeshi Garnish (see page 150), lemon wedges and chutneys.

BATTER
4 oz (110 g) gram flour (besan)
2 tablespoons chopped fresh coriander leaves
1 tablespoon bottled curry paste (see page 26)
1 teaspoon Bangladeshi Garam Masala (see page 34)

1 teaspoon ground cummin
a pinch of asafoetida (hing)
1 teaspoon salt

8 oz (225 g) onions (1 large Spanish onion), chopped into fine 1 inch (2.5 cm) strips
vegetable oil for deep-frying

1. Mix the batter ingredients with enough water to achieve a thickish paste which will drop sluggishly off the spoon. Let it stand for at least 10 minutes, during which time the mixture will absorb the moisture.

2. Next add the onion. Mix in well and leave again for about 10 minutes to absorb the batter mixture.

3. Meanwhile, heat the deep-frying oil to 375°F/190°C. This temperature is below smoking point and will cause a sliver of batter to splutter a bit, then float more or less at once.

4. Inspect the mixture. There must be no 'powder' left. It must be well mixed. Then simply scoop out one-eighth of the mixture and place it carefully in the oil. Place all eight portions in, but allow about 20 seconds between each one so that the oil will maintain its temperature.

5. Deep-fry for 10–12 minutes, turning once. Remove from the oil, and drain well on kitchen paper.

Shobji Pakora

VEGETABLE FRIED FRITTERS

•

THIS is a variation on the previous onion *bhajia*, also from my *Curry Club Indian Vegetarian Cookbook* (see page ii), but using a different batter and a mixed vegetable filling. The difference between *pakora* and bhajia batter, according to my Bangladeshi friend Rasheed, is that the former has egg and white flour, the latter does not. It's a bit academic, I think, and you can use either batter for either recipe.

——— MAKES 8 pakora ———

BATTER

4 oz (110 g) gram flour (besan) or 2 oz (50 g) gram flour and 2 oz (50 g) plain flour

1 egg

3 oz (75 g) plain yoghurt

1 tablespoon fresh or bottled lemon juice

1 teaspoon salt

½ teaspoon lovage seeds (ajwain)

2 teaspoons Bangladeshi Garam Masala (see page 34)

2 teaspoons dried fenugreek leaves

½–2 teaspoons chilli powder

FILLING

4 oz (110 g) shredded carrot

2 oz (50 g) cooked green peas

2 oz (50 g) chopped spinach

1–2 fresh coriander leaves, finely chopped

vegetable oil for deep-frying

Follow the method for the previous recipe in its entirety.

OPPOSITE PREVIOUS PAGE Clockwise from top: *Kocchu* (green-leaf soup with patra leaves, spinach and rocket, page 53), *Alu Chop* (mince-filled potato cutlet, page 42) *Shinghara* (conical-shaped stuffed pastry with vegetable filling, page 48), all with a Bangladeshi garnish of cucumber slices, lime wedges and green chillies (page 150)

OPPOSITE Clockwise from top: *Razma Dal* (red kidney bean curry, page 130), *Morog Pakora Narish* (Narish's Batter-coated Chicken, page 79) and *Morichi Dhana Sag* (green chilli and coriander leaf relish, page 151). The green vegetable at the top of the picture is a *chichinga* (page 123)

Tok Dal Jhol

BANGLADESHI SOUR LENTIL SOUP

•

SOUR tastes are adored by Bangladeshis. Tamarind is a delicious souring agent and is used in this traditional dish. *Tok Dal Jhol* is very nutritious and cheap and although it is offered here as a soup, it could just as well be served with plain rice to make a satisfying main course meal. See also Tok Dhal on page 132.

──────── SERVES 4 ────────

4 oz (110 g) red massor lentils, split and polished
3 tablespoons tamarind purée (see page 38)
3 tablespoons mustard blend oil
3–4 garlic cloves, crushed
4 oz (110 g) onion, chopped
2–3 tomatoes, chopped
2–3 fresh green cayenne chillies, sliced longways

several fresh coriander leaves, chopped
a little sugar to taste (optional)
salt to taste

SPICES
½ teaspoon turmeric
1 teaspoon Panch Foran (see page 36)
2–3 bay leaves
1–2 teaspoons chopped dry red chillies

1. Pick through the lentils to remove any grit or impurities. Rinse them several times, then drain and soak in ample water for 4 hours (see note).

2. Drain and rinse the lentils then add them and the tamarind purée to 1¾ pints (1 litre) water, already at the simmer in a 4 pint (2.25 litre) saucepan.

3. While the lentils cook, heat the oil in a karahi or wok. Stir-fry the **spices** for 3 seconds, add the garlic and stir-fry for 30 seconds more. Then add the onion, tomato and green chillies. Simmer for about 8–10 minutes to achieve a tarka (see page 31).

4. Add the fried ingredients to the saucepan at any time.

5. The soup will need about 45 minutes to simmer.

6. Just prior to serving, add the chopped coriander leaves, sugar if liked and salt to taste.

NOTE
The 4 hour soak can be omitted but you will need to simmer for longer and may have to add more water during cooking.

Kocchu

GREEN LEAF SOUP

•

JUST 7 kilometres outside bustling, congested, steaming hot Sylhet, is the 56 acre Burgan tea garden. We visited the factory and plantation at its busy time. Ancient machines from Belfast, Manchester and Ipswich still mince the leaves and dry, grade and pack them, operating as well as the day they were installed 60 years ago.

The plantation is now owned by the delightful and gentle Professor Shafique, whose philosophy enchanted us. He talked of Bangladesh's problems of starvation. 'All around us, growing wild is the kocchu leaf. It is prolific, rich in iron and most enjoyable to eat. Yet people choose to starve or pay at market for farmers' crops, rather than eat what is there for all, for no money.'

Whilst he talked a small bowl of thick, dark green liquid was served. It was kocchu soup, and it was outstandingly tasty. *Kocchu* is Bangladeshi for green colocasia, or *dasheen* leaves, from a tuber called taro (*Colocasia esculenta*). The deep green, heart-shaped, velvety, soft leaves are about 6 inches (15 cm) long, supported by a long stem. In Hindi/Urdu they are called *arvi sag* or *patia*; in Gujarat it is *patra*, and in the West Indies, *callaloo*. They are often available at Asian and West Indian stores (try all the names!). If you cannot get them, a delicate and acceptable substitute is rocket.

─────── SERVES 4 (small quantities) ───────

10 oz (300 g) green colocasia leaves or young rocket leaves	a pinch of turmeric
2 teaspoons mustard blend oil	a pinch of sugar
⅓ teaspoon very finely chopped garlic	⅔ teaspoon tamarind purée (see page 38)
1 oz (25 g) onion, very finely chopped	salt to taste
	lime wedges to serve

1. Remove the stems from the leaves. Then either steam or microwave them just enough to soften them.

2. Mince the leaves as finely as you can, discarding any pithy ribs. Re-steam or microwave again until they are quite soft, then force them through a sieve.

3. Heat the oil. Stir-fry the garlic, onion, turmeric, sugar and tamarind. Add the sieved leaves and just enough water to make the mixture quite loose but not too runny.

4. Get the leaves warm, not hot. Salt to taste and serve warm (or cold) with the lime wedges.

Ponchar Tok

SOUR MEAT SOUP

•

THIS is a stock or soup that uses meat or poultry bones. It is popular in Sylhet, mainly because it is chilli-hot and very sour (*tok* is Sylhetti for 'sour'). There they use a grapefruit-like fruit, called *shaktora* to create the sourness. This is not too dissimilar from the West Indian *shaddock* (or *pommelo*) and both shaktora and shaddock can be bought in the United Kingdom. If both are unavailable try a mixture of grapefruit and lime. Here I have used lamb chops, not really a Bangladeshi meat cut, but it works very well. Oxtail does too, and is cheap. Ask your butcher.

Serve on its own or with plain rice.

———— SERVES 4 ————

1 shaktora or ½ grapefruit and ½ lime
2 tablespoons butter ghee
2 tablespoons vegetable oil
3 garlic cloves, finely chopped
4 oz (110 g) onion, finely chopped
1–2 teaspoons chopped dry red chillies
10 oz (300 g) small, lean lamb chops or chopped trimmed oxtail
4 fl oz (110 ml) home-made yoghurt (see page 33)

2–3 fresh green chillies, sliced longways
1 tablespoon chopped fresh coriander leaves
a little sugar to taste (optional)
salt to taste

SPICES
½ teaspoon turmeric
1 teaspoon Bangladeshi Garam Masala (see page 34)
1 teaspoon Panch Foran (see page 36)

1. Peel the shaktora and chop up and use all its peel, which is quite edible. Chop the segments into halves. Or peel the grapefruit and lime, discarding all but about one-sixth of the peel (large bits).

2. Heat the ghee and oil in a saucepan. Add the garlic and **spices** and stir-fry for a minute. Add the onion and dry red chilli and sizzle on a lower heat for 5 minutes or more, stirring occasionally.

3. During this, cut away the meat from the bones of the lamb chops, discarding any unwanted matter such as fat and gristle.

4. Add the bones and meat to the saucepan, raise the heat and stir-fry for about 5 minutes more.

5. Over the next 10 minutes, add 1⅓ pints (800 ml) water and the yoghurt in, say, four equal batches, stirring as necessary. Obtain a rolling simmer which will maintain a good 'bhoona' (see page 28).

6. Add the shaktora or grapefruit and lime, and gently simmer, lid on, for 30 minutes more.

7. The mixture should be quite soup-like and not too thick by now. Add the green chillies, chopped coriander leaves, sugar if liked and salt to taste.

—— *Variations* ——

Shaktora Gusht (Citrus-flavoured meat) Another highly popular Sylhetti dish is Shaktora Gusht, literally 'sour-tasting meat curry'. To achieve this, simply use more lamb chops or oxtail – up to 1 lb (450 g) – and halve the water. Keep everything else the same.

Ponchar Khatta   In Bangladesh an even sourer dish is made by adding 2 tablespoons Tamarind Purée (see page 38) at Step 4.

Borhani

SPICY YOGHURT DRINK

•

IN INDIA spicy, icy yoghurt drinks – *lhassi* – are popular and refreshing. But the Bangladeshi version has a wow factor I've never encountered in India. They add ground fresh chillies! Hot stuff indeed and just fantabulous on a hot day! But equally good at any time, especially using home-made yoghurt. Borhani is traditionally served with Tehari (see page 138).

—— SERVES 2 ——

10 fl oz (300 ml) home-made yoghurt (see
   page 33)
5 fl oz (150 ml) water
1 teaspoon chopped fresh mint
½ teaspoon ground cummin
½ teaspoon ground black pepper

½ teaspoon Bangladeshi Garam Masala (see
   page 34)
2–3 fresh green (or red) chillies, very finely
   chopped
crushed ice to serve

1. Whisk together everything but the crushed ice.

2. Serve with the crushed ice in two tall glasses.

CHAPTER 3

MEAT

 IN COMPLETE contrast to India, where the cow is too sacred to eat, beef is the primary meat in Bangladesh.

In one sense this is good news for us in the West because our beef is so prolific and tender. However, that also creates a slight problem. Bangladeshi cattle are much smaller, yielding only one-fifth as much meat as their American or British counterparts (and only one-thirty-second as much milk). And their meat is much tougher, too. This requires meat-tenderising techniques and much longer cooking times than we need. I have taken that into account in the recipes. Meat is always enjoyed on the bone in Bangladesh as bone, especially with marrow, adds flavour to gravy. Our meat cuts tend to leave bones whole, whereas they are better for currying if cross-cut into sections (the butcher will oblige) with meat attached.

There are more goats than cattle in Bangladesh (30 million as opposed to 23 million) but a goat yields far less meat than a cow. By comparison there are only one million sheep, so mutton is a rare treat and lamb even more so – again in contrast to India where sheep (and goats) are the main sources of meat.

Until the arrival of the Moslems in the twelfth century and their prohibition on eating pork, this meat was very popular in the Bengal area. However, after the Moslem invasion its popularity declined until the British arrived in the nineteenth century. Today wild boar are not uncommon and are occasionally eaten by both Hindus and Christians. However, given the Moslem majority in Bangladesh (87 per cent), I have omitted recipes that use pork although it could be substituted in most of the recipes.

So, too, could venison. Various types of deer are not uncommon in Bangladesh, especially in the forested areas around Sylhet.

Nothing curries better than meat, as these recipes prove.

Shami Kebab Sonargaon

MEAT PATTIES

•

BANGLADESH'S capital Dhaka is home to its top hotel, the Sonargaon. It's as glossy and costly a place as you'll find anywhere, and so is the food.

At its Karwan Sarai restaurant we came across this silky, chic sheek *kebab*, which we were told was a 'gift from Moghul times'. The silky secret lies in simmering the mince with lentils and then regrinding it as finely as possible, with pâté.

Serve with Bangladeshi Garnish (see page 150) and chutneys.

─────── MAKES 8 ───────

2 oz (50 g) red massor lentils, split and polished
1 lb (450 g) very lean beef steak
2 garlic cloves, very finely chopped
1 inch (2.5 cm) piece fresh ginger, very finely chopped
2 tablespoons dried onion flakes, crumbled
6 tablespoons butter ghee
1 egg yolk
1 tablespoon finely chopped fresh coriander leaves
1–2 fresh green chillies, finely chopped

1 teaspoon salt
4 oz (110 g) finely ground pâté (any type)
some cornflour for dusting
1 egg, beaten

SPICES
1 teaspoon Bangladeshi Garam Masala (see page 34)
$\frac{1}{2}$ teaspoon ground black pepper
$\frac{1}{2}$ teaspoon ground coriander
$\frac{1}{4}$ teaspoon turmeric

1. Pick through the lentils to remove impurities, then wash and soak them for an hour or so.

2. Put the meat, garlic, ginger, dried onion and **spices** through a mincer, or food processor, with the lentils.

3. Heat the ghee in a large, flat frying pan. Add the mixture and stir-fry for about 20 minutes. Add water, spoonful by spoonful, to prevent it catching. But do not swamp it.

4. Take off the heat and strain off and reserve the ghee, which will be used later in Step 8. Allow the mixture to cool, thicken and dry. Leave it for at least 3 hours or, better, overnight.

5. Next day, or when ready, add the egg yolk, chopped coriander leaves, chillies and salt, and run once again through the mincer or food processor.

With luck you should now have a thickish, lump-free mouldable paste. To make sure, now add the pâté. If it is a little too thick add a splash of water.

6. Divide the mixture into eight.

7. Roll one portion into a ball, lightly dust it with cornflour then press it down to become a disc. Smooth it down then dip it in the beaten egg. Repeat with the other seven portions.

8. Heat the reserved ghee in a large, flat frying pan and fry for about 10–12 minutes, turning at least once, halfway.

Noorani Kebab

BEEF-ENCASED CHICKEN PATTY

•

SOME work to do for this one, but no one said it was easy to create the best dishes! And this is a really good one ... good enough to impress at a dinner party. And it is easy, but don't tell your guests. The hard work is mostly confined to pressing the food processor button and mixing things! The result is spicy, white chicken breast surrounded by red, beef kebab mince. It is oven-baked then sliced, Swiss roll style, and looks as pretty as it tastes.

It can be served as a starter with Bangladeshi Garnish (see page 150) and chutneys or as part of a main course.

———— SERVES 4 ————

6 oz (175 g) chicken breast fillets, skinned
6–8 fresh mint leaves, chopped
⅓ teaspoon salt
1 lb (450 g) very lean beef steak
2 garlic cloves, very finely chopped
4 tablespoons dried onion flakes
1 tablespoon finely chopped fresh coriander leaves
2–3 green chillies, shredded
½ teaspoon salt

SPICES I
1 teaspoon Panch Foran (see page 36)
1 teaspoon white pepper
1 teaspoon sesame seeds

SPICES 2
2 teaspoons Bangladeshi Garam Masala (see page 34)
1 teaspoon chilli powder
1 teaspoon paprika

1. Pre-heat the oven to 375°F/190°C/Gas Mark 5.

2. Roughly cut up the chicken breasts and mix them with the fresh mint, salt and **spices 1**. Pulse them in the food processor until well ground (or mince them). Remove from the processor.

3. Roughly cut up the steak mixing it with the garlic, onion, chopped coriander leaves, chillies, salt and **spices 2**. Pulse this through the food processor until well ground (or mince it).

4. Shape the by now very mouldable chicken into a thin sausage.

5. Cover the sausage with the mouldable beef, retaining its shape and achieving a smooth surface.

6. Put the sausage on a foil-lined oven tray, and place in the oven.

7. Bake for about 18–20 minutes.

8. Remove and allow to rest for a few minutes. Then cut it Swiss roll style.

Shuti Kebabs

BEEF PATTIES

•

BANGLADESH beef is generally tough, as I mentioned in this chapter's introduction. The way they tenderise their meat is to marinate it in green papaya or pawpaw, a tropical fruit. Here we don't need to do this (so I've called it optional). This dish was presented at a recent Bangladeshi Food Festival, at Amin Ali's Red Fort Restaurant in London, by Samir Uddin, the head chef to the former nawabs of Dhaka.

Serve with plain rice or a bread.

NOTE

Spice shops sell an alternative to papaya in packets called 'meat tenderiser'. It can be substituted for papaya or both can be omitted.

——— SERVES 4 ———

4 slices minute steak, each weighing about 5 oz (150 g)
1 tablespoon ground green papaya or meat tenderiser (optional)
5 fl oz (150 ml) home-made yoghurt (see page 33)
3 tablespoons butter ghee
½ teaspoon turmeric
4 garlic cloves, sliced
1 tablespoon chopped fresh coriander leaves

1 teaspoon Bangladeshi Garam Masala (see page 34)
salt to taste

SPICES

1 teaspoon white cummin seeds
½ teaspoon coriander seeds, crushed
½ teaspoon crushed black pepper
2 bay leaves
3–4 dry red chillies

1. Carefully beat the minute steaks so that they become enlarged. Sprinkle on or work in the ground papaya or meat tenderiser. Cut the steaks into strips about 1½ inches (3.75 cm) wide.

2. Mix the yoghurt and **spices** together in a large, non-metallic bowl. Put the strips in. Cover the bowl and put in the fridge for 24–60 hours.

3. To cook, heat the ghee in a karahi or wok. Stir-fry the turmeric for 10 seconds. Add the garlic and make a tarka (see page 31).

4. Add the meat and all the marinade and simmer gently for about 8 minutes.

5. Add the chopped coriander leaves, garam masala and salt to taste and, if at any time it needs it, enough water to keep the mixture from sticking.

6. Simmer for a few more minutes until it is as tender as you want it.

Kasa Kalia

RED BEEF CURRY

•

THE *kalia* style of curry-cooking is particular to Bengal and Bangladesh. Meat is traditionally its main subject, but poultry or fish kalia are also enjoyed. Red colours are mandatory, from the chillies and tomato. Spicing includes the popular poppy seeds.

Serve with a lentil and/or vegetable dish and a rice.

———— SERVES 4 ————

1½ lb (675 g) stewing steak, weighed after removing all unwanted matter
4 tablespoons butter ghee
2 garlic cloves, chopped
1 inch (2.5 cm) piece fresh ginger, very finely chopped
8 oz (225 g) onions, finely sliced
1 teaspoon chopped dry red chilli
1–2 fresh red chillies, sliced
2 teaspoons tomato purée
1 tablespoon tomato ketchup
4 oz (110 g) carrots, sliced

2 teaspoons Bangladeshi Garam Masala (see page 34)
1 teaspoon finely chopped fresh coriander leaves
salt to taste

SPICES

1 teaspoon white cummin seeds
¼ teaspoon coriander seeds, crushed
2 inch (5 cm) piece cassia bark
2–3 bay leaves
1 teaspoon white poppy seeds (posta dana)
½ teaspoon chilli powder
½ teaspoon turmeric

1. Cut the meat into suitable sized cubes and pre-heat the oven to 375°F/190°C/Gas Mark 5.

2. Heat the ghee in a karahi or wok. Add the garlic and stir-fry for 30 seconds. Add the ginger and continue for 30 seconds more. Add the **spices** and stir-fry for 30 seconds more. Add the onions and, lowering the heat, fry until they become a tarka (see page 31), adding splashes of water, if needed, to prevent sticking (see note).

3. Add the meat and stir-fry for 5 minutes.

4. Transfer the contents of the karahi into a lidded casserole dish, stirring in the chillies, tomato purée, ketchup and carrots. Put the dish in the oven.

5. After 20 minutes inspect and stir, adding a little water if needed. Cook for 20 minutes more. Test for tenderness – it should be nearly there. Add the garam masala, chopped coriander leaves and salt to taste. Cook for a final 15–20 minutes by which time the meat should be really tender.

Gomangse Bhoona

SLOW FRIED BEEF CURRY

•

ON PAGE 28 we saw how to *bhoona* spices. The process is also used to cook meat curries. For it to be truly successful, it needs rather more oil or ghee than you would wish to eat with the dish, which is why restaurant curries are sometimes served swimming in oil.

In fact, as soon as the bhoona has achieved its purpose – to reduce out or remove all moisture – the oil separates and 'floats' above the cooked food. From that point onwards water or liquids can be introduced without spoiling the flavour of the cooked spices.

One final observation about the bhoona: spoon off as much of the excess oil as you can prior to serving. I can't emphasise that enough. Though slightly 'tainted' and coloured, it will be clear and perfectly good to use again (and again), so store it for the next curry.

In this delightful and authentic Bangladeshi bhoona, which appears in the cover photograph, notice how few initial spices are used to create the fragrant tastes.

——— SERVES 4 ———

1½ lb (675 g) stewing steak, weighed after removing all unwanted matter
10 tablespoons butter ghee
1 teaspoon turmeric
2 teaspoons ground coriander
1 teaspoon coriander seeds, crushed
3–4 × 2 inch (5 cm) pieces cassia bark
3–4 bay leaves
6–8 garlic cloves, finely chopped
2 inch (5 cm) piece fresh ginger, finely chopped
8 oz (225 g) onions, very finely chopped

4–6 fresh red cayenne chillies, sliced
up to 8 fl oz (250 ml) akhni stock (see page 38) or water
2 tablespoons chopped fresh coriander leaves
salt to taste

GARNISH
a sprinkling of Bangladeshi Garam Masala (see page 34), optional
toasted sliced almonds
Onion Tarka (see page 31)
fresh coriander leaves

1. Cut the meat into suitable sized cubes and pre-heat the oven to 375°F/190°C/Gas Mark 5.

2. Heat the ghee on the stove in a 4–5 pint (2.25–2.75 litre) flameproof casserole dish with a lid.

3. Add the turmeric and ground coriander and stir-fry for 30 seconds. Add the coriander seeds and cassia bark, bay leaves, garlic and ginger, lower the heat and obtain a golden brown tarka (see note) over about 5 minutes.

4. Add the onions and continue stir-frying on a low heat (just sizzling) to continue the tarka, taking around 15 minutes.

5. Add the meat and continue to stir-fry for about 10 minutes more, 'sealing' the meat. Add the chillies.

6. Put the lidded casserole into the oven.

7. After 20 minutes, inspect and stir. The meat should not be shrivelling or drying out. We want it to be juicy in a juicy gravy. Add just enough akhni stock or water to ensure this, now and throughout the remaining cooking, as needed.

8. Inspect again after 20 more minutes. Add the chopped coriander leaves and salt to taste. Return to the oven for a final 10 minutes by which time the meat should be really tender. (If it isn't quite tender, give it a little more oven time.)

9. Remove from the oven, stir and leave it to rest for about 10 minutes. Then spoon off all excess ghee and save it for another time.

10. Garnish with the garam masala if liked, nuts, onion tarka and fresh coriander leaves.

NOTE
Steps 3 and 4 can be reduced in time to less than a minute, if you use the pre-made tarkas described on pages 31 and 32.

Peshi Korma

CREAMY BEEF CURRY

•

This was originally a beef Moghul curry, cooked by the *bhoona* process, to which yoghurt and aromatic spices, but no turmeric or chilli, were added. Bangladeshi *kormas* can use cream in place of yoghurt or coconut milk, as we do here, and optionally they like to add turmeric to give the dish colour. And chillies are not unknown – in fact, I would say that chilli-loving Bangladeshis wouldn't make this dish without them!

Here, using beef (but you could use lamb or veal), is a truly Bangladeshi Moghul curry. Note the marinade – an important feature of the dish.

You can substitute yoghurt for the coconut milk, but use more water at Step 5; or use 6 fl oz (175 ml) single cream. All give different tastes, all are worth trying.

——— SERVES 4 ———

1½ lb (675 g) stewing steak, weighed after removing unwanted matter
14 fl oz (400 ml) tinned coconut milk
4–6 garlic cloves, very finely chopped
2 inch (5 cm) piece fresh ginger, very finely chopped
1 tablespoon brown sugar
1 teaspoon salt
10 tablespoons butter ghee
1 teaspoon turmeric
8 oz (225 g) onions, very finely chopped
1 fresh green chilli, cut into rings
1 tablespoon chopped fresh coriander leaves
2 teaspoons Bangladeshi Garam Masala (see page 34)
salt to taste

SPICES
½ teaspoon black cummin seeds
6–8 green cardamom pods, crushed
1 teaspoon coriander seeds, crushed
½ teaspoon cloves
2 inch (5 cm) piece cassia bark
½ teaspoon fennel seeds
2–3 bay leaves

GARNISH
chopped cashew nuts
Onion Tarka (see page 31)
fresh coriander leaves

1. Cut the meat into suitable sized cubes.

2. In a large, non-metallic bowl, mix together the coconut milk, garlic, ginger, sugar, salt and the **spices**. Add the meat, ensuring the cubes are well coated. Cover the bowl with film and place in the fridge for 24–60 hours (see page 17).

3. Pre-heat the oven to 375°F/190°C/Gas Mark 5.

4. Heat the ghee on the stove in a 4–5 pint (2.25–2.75 litre) flameproof casserole dish with a lid. Add the turmeric and stir-fry for 30 seconds. Lower the heat, add the onions and stir-fry (just sizzling) for around 15 minutes to obtain a tarka (see note).

5. Add the meat and its marinade and continue to stir-fry for about 10 minutes more, 'sealing' the meat. Add the chilli rings.

6. Put the lidded casserole into the oven.

7. After 20 minutes, inspect and stir. The meat will be quite juicy and the coconut milk will have made a creamy sauce. It is just possible it may need a little water to keep it this way, now and throughout the cooking.

8. Inspect again after 20 minutes. Add the chopped coriander leaves, garam masala and salt to taste. Return to the oven for a final 10 minutes by which time the meat should be really tender. (If it isn't quite tender, give it a little more oven time.)

9. Remove from the oven, stir and leave it to rest for about 10 minutes. Then spoon off all excess ghee and reserve for another time.

10. Garnish with the nuts, onion tarka and fresh coriander leaves.

NOTE
Step 3 can be reduced in time to less than a minute, if you use the pre-made tarkas described on pages 31 and 32.

Bhera Mansha Rezala

CREAMY LAMB CURRY

•

A VERY rich dish this – richer even than *korma*. It must contain no red colours. In fact, a natural grey look is acceptable. Yellow is optional (using saffron not turmeric). Fresh green chilli is mandatory. The richness is obtained from cream or, better still, tinned evaporated milk which tastes like hand-stirred Bangladeshi reduced milk (*kisha/koya*).

In Bangladesh, goat (*chagor*) would be used, or mutton (*chagaler mansha*). We can use those, though lamb (*bhera*) is more likely to be available in the West. Be prepared for the sweetness from the sugar and raisins. It is a taste beloved by Bangladeshis, but one which can be omitted if you prefer. Try to use rosewater (get only top quality) for a gorgeous fragrance.

──────── SERVES 4 ────────

1½ lb (675 g) lean lamb steaks, weighed after removing unwanted matter
14 oz (410 g) tinned evaporated milk
10 tablespoons butter ghee
10 garlic cloves, very finely chopped
8 oz (225 g) onions, very finely chopped
3–4 fresh green chillies, sliced longways
up to 6 fl oz (175 ml) akhni stock (see page 38) or water
1 tablespoon raisins (optional)
2 teaspoons sugar
2 tablespoons chopped pistachio nuts
1 tablespoon ground almonds
2 teaspoons Bangladeshi Garam Masala (see page 34)

salt to taste
2 tablespoons rosewater
20–30 strands saffron (optional)

SPICES
12 green cardamom pods, crushed
3–4 × 2 inch (5 cm) pieces cassia bark
2 teaspoons Panch Foran (see page 36)

GARNISH
a curl of cream
fresh coriander leaves
green chilli rings
toasted almond slices

1. Cut the lamb into suitable sized cubes and put in a bowl with the evaporated milk. Pre-heat the oven to 375°F/190°C/Gas Mark 5.

2. Heat the ghee on the stove in a 4–5 pint (2.25–2.75 litre) flameproof casserole dish with a lid. Add the **spices** and stir-fry for 30 seconds. Lower the heat and add the garlic, stir-frying to obtain a golden brown tarka (see note) over about 5 minutes.

3. Add the onions and continue stir-frying on a low heat (just sizzling) to continue the tarka, taking around 15 minutes.

4. Add the meat/milk mixture and the chillies to the casserole and, when sizzling, put the lidded casserole into the oven.

5. After 20 minutes, inspect and stir. The meat should not be shrivelling or drying out. We want it to be juicy in a juicy gravy. Add just enough akhni stock or water to ensure this, now and throughout the remaining cooking, as needed.

6. Inspect again after 20 minutes. Add the raisins, sugar, pistachio nuts, ground almonds, garam masala and salt to taste. It should now be quite thickly creamy. Return to the oven for a final 10 minutes by which time the meat should be really tender. (If it isn't quite tender, give it a little more oven time.)

7. Remove from the oven, stir and leave it to rest for about 10 minutes. Then spoon off all excess ghee and reserve for another time. Stir in the rosewater, and saffron if you want a hint of yellow, and serve garnished with a curl of cream, the fresh coriander leaves, chilli rings and almonds.

NOTE
Steps 2 and 3 can be reduced in time to less than a minute, if you use the pre-made tarkas described on pages 31 and 32.

Gol Alu Gosht

MEAT WITH POTATOES

•

THE notion of incorporating large chunks of potato with meat and slowly currying them is widespread in Bangladesh. It is not only economical, it is also effective with the potato absorbing flavours whilst cooking. It's popular at the curry restaurant too, but this recipe gives you the authentic Bangladeshi tastes, using bones and all. I insist that you don't leave the bones out (see the introduction to this chapter). Get the butcher to cut them into small pieces. Note again how a minimal number of spices achieves maximum taste. The actual spices used here are a traditional Bengali mix called '*dana-zira*'. Its flavours are composed mainly of coriander (*dana*) and cummin (*zira*).

──────── SERVES 4 ────────

1 lb (450 g) stewing steak
3 large potatoes
8 tablespoons butter ghee
10 garlic cloves, very finely chopped
8 oz (225 g) onions, very finely chopped
8 oz (225 g) chopped beef leg bones
2–3 green chillies, sliced
up to 6 fl oz (175 ml) akhni stock (see page 38) or water
3 tablespoons chopped fresh coriander leaves
salt to taste

SPICES (dana-zira)
$2\frac{1}{2}$ teaspoons ground coriander
$2\frac{1}{2}$ teaspoons ground cummin
1 teaspoon ground black pepper
1 teaspoon turmeric
$\frac{1}{4}$ teaspoon asafoetida

GARNISH
2 teaspoons roasted white cummin seeds
fresh coriander leaves

1. Cut the meat into suitable sized cubes and pre-heat the oven to 375°F/190°C/Gas Mark 5.

2. Peel and quarter the potatoes.

3. Heat the ghee on the stove in a 4–5 pint (2.25–2.75 litre) flameproof casserole dish with a lid. Add the **spices** and stir-fry for 30 seconds. Add the garlic and lower the heat to obtain a golden brown tarka (see note) over about 5 minutes.

4. Add the onions and continue stir-frying on a low heat (just sizzling) to continue the tarka, taking around 15 minutes.

5. Add the meat and bones and continue to stir-fry for about 10 more minutes, 'sealing' the meat. Add the potatoes and chillies.

6. Put the lidded casserole into the oven.

7. After 20 minutes, inspect and stir. The meat should not be shrivelling or drying out. We want it to be juicy in a juicy gravy. Add just enough akhni stock or water to ensure this, now and throughout the remaining cooking, as needed.

8. Inspect again after 20 minutes. Add the chopped coriander leaves and salt to taste. Return to the oven for a final 10 minutes, by which time the meat should be really tender. (If it isn't quite tender, give it a little more oven time.)

9. Remove from the oven, stir and leave it to rest for about 10 minutes. Then spoon off all excess ghee and reserve for another time.

10. Garnish with the cummin seeds and fresh coriander leaves.

NOTE
Steps 3 and 4 can be reduced in time to less than a minute, if you use the pre-made tarkas described on pages 31 and 32.

Savar Pasanda

BEATEN MEDALLIONS OF BEEF

•

POPULAR at the restaurant, *pasanda* is served in a creamy sauce. This authentic version from the Dhaka Sheraton hotel uses beaten beef fillet medallions, from cattle reared in the nearby town of Savar, home to the imposing national martyrs' memorial which was built to commemorate Bangladesh's war of independence in 1971. Savar is also home to a large government-run dairy farm. Nearby is a huge, bustling cattle market, acres across, where endlessly frantic trading takes place. All day long the cattle arrive and depart in open trucks, neatly and comfortably packed in three rows of six. The best Bangladeshi breed for meat are a healthy looking tan or grey-white cattle with upright horns, called *shahiwal*. Any tender beef will do, but choice fully trimmed fillet steaks are undoubtedly the best for this dish. Veal escalopes are also good.

――― SERVES 4 ―――

1½ lb (675 g) lean fillet steak or veal escalope, weighed after trimming all unwanted matter
30 white cashew nuts, chopped
10 tablespoons butter ghee
4–6 garlic cloves, very finely chopped
8 oz (225 g) onions, very finely chopped
7 fl oz (200 ml) single cream
akhni stock (see page 38) or water
1 tablespoon very finely chopped fresh coriander leaves
salt to taste

SPICES I
2 tablespoons coriander seeds

1 tablespoon green cardamom seeds
1 teaspoon brown cardamom seeds

SPICES 2
1 teaspoon turmeric
1 teaspoon chilli powder
1 teaspoon white pepper
½ teaspoon ground cinnamon
¼ teaspoon ground coriander
2 teaspoons sugar

GARNISH
fresh coriander leaves
Onion Tarka (see page 31)
toasted almond slices, crumbled

1. The steaks or escalopes must be beaten a little. Sandwich them in film or foil and gently tap them with a meat mallet until they flatten to about half the thickness they were. Cut into strips.

2. Pre-heat the oven to 375°F/190°C/Gas Mark 5.

3. Roast and grind **spices 1** with the cashew nuts and enough water to make a thickish paste.

4. Heat the ghee on the stove in a 4–5 pint (2.25–2.75 litre) flameproof casserole dish with a lid.

5. Add **spices 2** and stir-fry for 30 seconds. Add the garlic and stir-fry for a further minute (see note).

6. Add the onions and continue stir-frying on a low heat (just sizzling) to continue the tarka, taking around 15 minutes.

7. Add the spice paste, and stir-fry it for a couple of minutes. Add the cream.

8. Put the lidded casserole into the oven.

9. After 20 minutes, inspect and stir. The meat should not be shrivelling or drying out. We want it to be juicy in a juicy gravy. Add just enough akhni stock or water to ensure this, now and throughout the remaining cooking, as needed.

10. Inspect again after 20 minutes. Add the chopped coriander leaves and salt to taste. Return to the oven for a final 10 minutes, by which time the meat should be really tender. (If it isn't quite tender, give it a little more oven time.)

11. Remove from the oven, stir and leave it to rest for about 10 minutes. Then spoon off all excess ghee and reserve for another time.

12. Garnish with the fresh coriander leaves, onion tarka and toasted almonds.

NOTE
Steps 5 and 6 can be reduced in time to less than a minute, if you use the pre-made tarkas described on pages 31 and 32.

Mojoj Kalia

BRAIN CURRY

•

Each of my curry books (see page ii) contains at least one 'exotic' recipe, and this book is no exception. Brain curry is considered a treat in Bangladesh. Brain, a type of offal, is an acquired taste, having a light 'foamy' texture. The choice is between lamb's brain or calf's brain. Both are quite small (lamb's averages $\frac{1}{4}$ lb (125 g) and calf's 6 oz (175 g)). Get your butcher to trim the brain and dice it into $1\frac{1}{2}$ inch (3.75 cm) cubes.

Because it is cooked in the *kalia* method it must have red colours, and these include red chillies and tomatoes and red pepper.

As this is such a specialist dish, I have portioned it for two assuming it will be served with other curries, rice and breads.

─────── SERVES 2 ───────

12 oz (350 g) trimmed and diced lamb or calf brain (see above)
1 tablespoon Tamarind Purée (see page 38)
1 tablespoon tomato purée
4–6 garlic cloves, chopped
4 tablespoons butter ghee
1 teaspoon white cummin seeds
1–2 fresh red chillies, chopped
1 tablespoon chopped red bell pepper
1 tablespoon tomato ketchup
2–3 tinned tomatoes, chopped
1 teaspoon Bangladeshi Garam Masala (see page 34)

2 teaspoons chopped fresh coriander leaves
salt to taste

SPICES 1
$\frac{1}{2}$ teaspoon ground coriander
$\frac{1}{2}$ teaspoon paprika
$\frac{1}{3}$ teaspoon cinnamon powder
$\frac{1}{2}$ teaspoon chilli powder
$\frac{1}{3}$ teaspoon turmeric

SPICES 2
1–2 bay leaves
2 teaspoons white poppy seeds

1. Wash the brain pieces thoroughly, then soak them in cold salty water for an hour to leech out possible bitter tastes. Wash again and set aside.

2. Roast **spices 1** and grind them with the tamarind and tomato purées, garlic and enough water to achieve a thick pourable paste.

3. Heat the ghee in a karahi or wok. Add the cummin seeds and stir-fry for 30 seconds. Lower the heat and add the paste. Stir-fry for 3–4 minutes.

4. Add a little water to keep things mobile. Add the brain and **spices 2**. Stir-fry for 3–4 minutes more.

5. Add the chillies, pepper, tomato ketchup and tomatoes and stir-fry for 6–8 minutes more, keeping a good water balance.

6. Add the garam masala and chopped coriander leaves, and salt to taste. Simmer for a few more minutes. Test that the brain is cooked (if not, go on until it is).

Boti Kebabs

MARINATED GRILLED VEAL PIECES

•

THE marinade is astonishingly basic, using just chilli powder, salt and garlic in yoghurt. But the taste is terrific. You can marinate the cubes for up to 60 hours (see page 17) covered in the fridge ... the longer the better (the minimum effective time is 24 hours).

Serve with Bangladeshi Garnish (see page 150) and chutneys.

——— SERVES 4 as a starter ———

1 lb (450 g) lean leg of veal, weighed after
  Step 1
1 tablespoon mustard blend oil
4 fl oz (110 ml) home-made yoghurt (see
  page 33)

4 garlic cloves, very finely chopped
3–4 teaspoons chilli powder
1 teaspoon salt
freshly ground black pepper to serve

1. Cut the veal into decent-sized cubes.

2. Mix the other ingredients together in a non-metallic bowl.

3. Add the cubes of veal and ensure they are well coated.

4. Cover the bowl with cling film and put in the fridge for 24–60 hours (see above).

5. To cook, heat the grill to medium, put the meat on a foil-lined grill-pan rack and put the rack into the midway position.

6. Grill for about 8 minutes. Turn the cubes over and grill for 6–7 minutes more.

7. Sprinkle with the black pepper.

CHAPTER 4

POULTRY

 ACCORDING to statistical information gathered by Dr Jahangir Alam of Bangladesh Agricultural University, there were 116.48 million chickens in Bangladesh in 1994. By the same token there were, it appears, 13.47 million ducks. These two figures are remarkable for their accuracy. Bangladesh's 1994 human population is quoted at between 105 and 125 million in various government publications. One wonders how poultry are counted to within 10,000 whilst the human count is accurate only to within 20 million!

Most chickens and ducks are owned by small farmer villagers, who are content to let their birds scavenge for a living in return for eggs and meat. The number of Bangladeshi specialist poultry-rearing units is rapidly increasing and the size of birds, though still much smaller than their Western counterparts (many are bantams), is increasing as breeding techniques improve.

Generally speaking the entire bird, jointed but on the bone, is used in recipes (after skinning and gutting); and with such a scarcity of birds, it is rarer to eat poultry than meat.

It is the reverse in the West, where chicken (and duck) is plentiful, inexpensive and considered more 'healthy' than red meat. Our enormous, filleted, skinned chicken breasts are, of course, perfect for all curries. But let's not forget how good legs, drumsticks and whole birds are – recipes in this chapter use them too, bones and all.

Eggs are enjoyed in Bangladeshi curries, and this is recognised in the Anday Dopeyaja recipe on page 88.

I have not included any game recipes in this book, but with Bangladesh's vast amount of water, wild duck and geese are easily hunted. So are partridge, pheasant and quail. The domestic chicken's ancient ancestor, the flashy red jungle fowl (*Gallus gallus*) – population unknown – is commonly encountered in wooded areas (and why do they dash suicidally across the roads?). Called *bahn morog*, it too is hunted and is popular. Guinea fowl can be substituted, and any game can be used in these recipes.

Jhalfri Morog
STIR-FRY CHICKEN CURRY
•

In the Chittagong hills a Buddhist tribe called the *mogs* can still be found. In the Anglo-Indian days of the Raj, mogs became household cooks, and between them and their British memsahibs they created Anglo-Indian food. One typical dish was called *jhalfri* (or *jhal firezee/farajee/freyzi*). It was a spicy stir-fry (or dry-fry) using cold leftover meat or chicken. I well remember my granny's versions.

But *jhalfri* (pronounced 'jarl-fry') can be used to cook fresh ingredients – none better than chicken. The resulting curry is rapidly cooked, fresh and sparkling.

It is known at the curry restaurant as *jal frezi*, where it has become almost as popular as chicken *tikka masala*. It was a thrill to find it native to Bangladesh, where they heap in the chillies.

It's one of my absolute favourites (which is why versions appear in my other curry books – see page ii), and if it isn't already yours it could be in just 20 minutes (the time it takes to cook)!

Serve with bread or fluffy plain rice.

―――― SERVES 4 ――――

1½ lb (675 g) chicken breasts, boned and skinned

4 tablespoons ghee or vegetable oil

2 teaspoons white cummin seeds

4 garlic cloves, finely chopped

2 inch (5 cm) piece fresh ginger, finely chopped

1 large Spanish onion, peeled and chopped

2–4 green chillies, sliced longways

1 tablespoon chopped green bell pepper

1 tablespoon chopped red bell pepper

2–3 tinned tomatoes, chopped

3 tablespoons coconut milk powder

2 teaspoons Bangladeshi Garam Masala (see page 34)

2 tablespoons chopped fresh coriander leaves

salt to taste

lemon juice to serve

SPICES

1 teaspoon paprika

½ teaspoon turmeric

2 teaspoons ground coriander

1 teaspoon ground cummin

1 teaspoon curry powder (see page 26)

½ teaspoon chilli powder

1. Cut the chicken breasts into bite-sized chunks.

2. Heat the ghee or oil in a karahi or wok. Stir-fry the cummin seeds for a few seconds. Add the garlic and continue stir-frying for 30 seconds. Add the ginger and continue for a minute. Add the **spices** and a splash of water, and stir-fry for a further minute.

3. Add the onion and stir-fry for at least 5 minutes.

4. Now add the chicken pieces and stir until they are evenly coloured yellow and are lightly sizzling. Add the chillies, peppers and tomatoes and stir-fry for 10 minutes. During this stage, add the coconut milk powder, spoonful by spoonful, to maintain a good liquid level.

5. Add the garam masala, chopped coriander leaves and salt to taste, then stir-fry for a final 5–10 minutes. Check that the chicken is cooked through, then serve at once, with a squeeze of lemon juice.

Morog Jal Do Peyaja
STIR-FRY CHICKEN CURRY WITH ONIONS
•

PEYAJA means 'onion'. *Do* means 'two'. Do pyazi is a typical Bengali dish in which onions appear in at least two forms.

This variation on the previous recipe incorporates more onion, in the form of spring onions. It is also somewhat wetter than regular *jal frezi*.

─── SERVES 4 ───

Add to the ingredients list of the previous recipe (Jhalfri Morog):
4–6 spring onions (bulbs and leaves), finely chopped

6–8 mint leaves, chopped
4 fl oz (100 ml) akhni stock (see page 38) or water

Follow the previous recipe in its entirety, adding the spring onions, mint leaves and stock or water at the beginning of Step 5.

Morog Pakora Narish
NARISH'S BATTER-COATED CHICKEN
•

WE WERE treated to this dish at the Sylhetti home of our friend Rasheed's sister, Narish. I've had chicken *pakora* several times before, but always with filleted cubes of breast. This was different. Narish had used drumsticks.

The drumstick is the lower leg of the fowl, below the knee and above the ankle, and is shaped more like a pestle than a drumstick. You should scrape away the flesh at the bone end to make it easier to handle. Made into a pakora, it is a neat package, and very tasty.

This recipe could be used for starters, or as part of a main course. Use the drumsticks from small birds. The double poussin, aged between 6 and 10 weeks is perfect. But the drumsticks of any small game bird (grouse, partridge, pigeon, even tiny quail) would be ideal.

Serve with a wet curry or two and rice or, if as a starter with Bangladeshi Garnish (see page 150), lemon wedges and chutneys.

———— SERVES 4 as a starter or part of a main course ————

4 small chicken drumsticks, skinned, pared at the bone (see above), washed and dried
oil for deep-frying

BATTER
4 oz (110 g) gram flour (besan) or 2 oz (50 g) gram flour and 2 oz (50 g) plain flour
1 egg

3 oz (75 g) plain yoghurt
1 tablespoon fresh or bottled lemon juice
1 teaspoon salt
$\frac{1}{2}$ teaspoon lovage seeds (ajwain)
2 teaspoons Bangladeshi Garam Masala (see page 34)
2 teaspoons dried fenugreek leaves
$\frac{1}{2}$–2 teaspoons chilli powder

1. Mix the batter ingredients to achieve a thickish paste which will drop sluggishly off the spoon. Let it stand for at least 10 minutes, during which time the mixture will absorb the moisture.

2. Meanwhile, heat the deep-frying oil to 375°F/190°C. This temperature is below smoking point and will cause a sliver of batter to splutter a bit, then float more or less at once.

3. Inspect the mixture. There must be no 'powder' left. It must be well mixed. Coat the drumsticks with the batter.

4. Carefully lower one drumstick into the oil. Place the others in, allowing about 20 seconds between each to maintain the temperature of the oil.

5. Deep-fry for 12–15 minutes, turning a few times. Remove from the oil, drain well on kitchen paper.

Morog Tikka

CHICKEN TIKKA

•

THE *tandoori* originated in the north-west of India centuries ago. Cooked in a large clay oven, it is not made in many homes on the subcontinent, especially those of Bangladesh. But it is available in restaurants there and is a popular occasional treat. It is even more popular in the United Kingdom, available at every Bangladeshi curry house. I feel quite at liberty, therefore, to include this recipe in this cookbook, and I make no apology for reproducing it from my book *Curry Club 100 Favourite Tandoori Recipes*.

Serve with Bangladeshi Garnish (see page 150), bread and chutneys.

———— SERVES 4 as a starter ————

1½ lb (675 g) chicken breasts, skinned, filleted and cut into 20–24 × 1½ inch (3.75 cm) cubes

MARINADE

2 teaspoons paprika
2 teaspoons chilli powder
2 teaspoons ground coriander
2 teaspoons Bangladeshi Garam Masala (see page 34)
1 teaspoon ground cummin

½ teaspoon turmeric
5 fl oz (150 ml) home-made yoghurt (see page 33)
2 tablespoons mustard blend oil
4 garlic cloves, very finely chopped
2 tablespoons freshly squeezed lemon juice
1 tablespoon tomato purée
1 teaspoon salt
about 2 fl oz (50 ml) milk (maybe more, maybe less)

1. Mix the marinade ingredients together in a large, non-metallic bowl.

2. Add the chicken pieces. Cover with cling film and refrigerate for 24–60 hours (see page 17).

3. Just prior to cooking divide the chicken between four skewers. (Use the spare marinade in a curry or discard it.)

4. Pre-heat the grill to medium. Place the skewers on an oven rack above a foil-lined grill tray and place the tray in the midway position. Alternatively, the chicken can be barbecued.

5. Cook for 5 minutes, turn, then cook for a further 5 minutes.

6. Cut through one piece of chicken to ensure that it is fully cooked – it should be white right through with no hint of pink. If not, cook for a while longer. When fully cooked, raise the tray nearer to the heat and singe the pieces to obtain a little blackening.

Morog Tikka Mossala

CHICKEN TIKKA MASALA

•

THE best hotel in Sylhet is called the Polash. It's a typical Indo-Bangladeshi hotel, frequented by businessmen. Its first claim to fame is that the owner has two Polash restaurants in Essex. Its second claim to fame is the remarkable 200 dish menu at its restaurant, the Shapnil. Dish number 95 immediately attracted my attention. It is for chicken *tikka masala*. 'And it is our most popular dish, just as it is in England,' said Polash owner Sheik Faruque Ahmed.

'We have another claim to fame,' he went on. 'We do takeaways. We can't get the foil containers so we use plastic bags.' Asked whether he got much business in a town full of curry restaurant owners, all of whom have cooks and servants in their large houses, Mr Ahmed said, 'No problem, business is booming, especially dish number 95.'

—— SERVES 4 ——

2 tablespoons vegetable oil
3 garlic cloves, finely chopped
8 oz (225 g) onions, very finely chopped
1½ tablespoons bottled mild curry paste (see page 26)
1½ tablespoons bottled tandoori paste (see page 26)
20–24 chicken tikka pieces, cooked to the recipe on page 80
6 tinned plum tomatoes, chopped

1 tablespoon vinegar, any type
1 tablespoon tomato ketchup
6 fl oz (175 ml) canned tomato soup
½ green pepper, chopped
0–4 fresh green chillies (optional)
4 fl oz (100 ml) single cream
1 tablespoon Bangladeshi Garam Masala (see page 34)
1 tablespoon chopped fresh coriander leaves
salt to taste

1. Heat the oil in a large karahi or wok.

2. Stir-fry the garlic for 30 seconds, then add the onions and stir-fry for 8–10 minutes until golden brown.

3. Add the pastes and stir-fry for a couple of minutes, then add the chicken and stir-fry for about 2 minutes, adding just enough water to keep things from sticking.

4. Add the tomatoes, vinegar, ketchup, soup, green pepper and chillies if using. Stir-fry for 5 minutes or so.

5. Then add the cream, garam masala and chopped coriander leaves. Simmer for a further 2 minutes, adding a little water if needed. Salt to taste and serve.

Morog Bhoona Anarosh
CHICKEN CURRY WITH PINEAPPLE
•

PINEAPPLES were brought to India by the Portuguese from Latin America as early as the sixteenth century. The Moghul emperor Shah Jehan adored them so much that they were grown, with difficulty, in the royal gardens in Agra. However, pineapples preferred the more humid temperatures of Bengal and to this day vast plantations exist north of Sylhet. Bengalis, with their sweet tooth, adored the Persian–influenced Moghul court dishes which incorporated fruit with meat or poultry. This one became a favourite at the Sylhetti court outstation, and no doubt with the emperor back in Agra. The notion of putting fruit in curry gripped early English travellers and, to this day, has resulted in appalling concoctions being meted out.

Done properly, the result is totally the reverse of appalling – it is quite unexpectedly subtle.

———— SERVES 4 ————

$1\frac{1}{2}$ lb (675 g) chicken legs, weighed after
    Step 1
10 tablespoons ghee
1 teaspoon coriander seeds, crushed
1 inch (2.5 cm) piece cassia bark
3–4 bay leaves
8–10 garlic cloves, finely chopped
8 oz (225 g) onions, very finely chopped
2–4 fresh green cayenne chillies, sliced
1 tablespoon chopped red bell pepper
up to 8 fl oz (225 ml) akhni stock (see page
    38) or water
3 tablespoons coconut milk powder
8 bite-sized cubes fresh pineapple
salt to taste
1 tablespoon chopped fresh coriander leaves

SPICES

1 teaspoon turmeric
2 teaspoons ground coriander
1 teaspoon ground cummin
1 teaspoon ground cinnamon
$\frac{1}{2}$ teaspoon ground cloves
3–4 bay leaves
8 green cardamom pods, crushed

GARNISH

Bangladeshi Garam Masala (see page 34)
toasted almonds
Onion Tarka (see page 31)
fresh coriander leaves

1. Skin the chicken legs, joint them and cut into small 3 inch (7.5 cm) pieces, on the bone. Your butcher will do this.

2. Pre-heat the oven to 375°F/190°C/Gas Mark 5.

3. Heat the ghee on the stove in a 4–5 pint (2.25–2.75 litre) flameproof casserole dish with a lid.

4. Add the **spices** and stir-fry for 30 seconds, then add the coriander seeds, cassia bark, bay leaves and garlic. Lower the heat and obtain a golden brown tarka (see note) over about 5 minutes.

5. Add the onions and continue stir-frying on a low heat (just sizzling) to continue the tarka, taking around 15 minutes.

6. Add the chicken pieces and continue to stir-fry for about 5 minutes, 'sealing' the meat. Add the chillies and pepper.

7. Put the lidded casserole into the oven.

8. After 15 minutes, inspect and stir. The chicken should not be shrivelling or drying out. We want it to be juicy in a juicy gravy. Add just enough akhni stock or water to ensure this, now and throughout the remaining cooking, as needed.

9. Inspect again after 15 minutes. Add the coconut milk powder, pineapple, salt to taste and chopped coriander leaves. Return to the oven for a final 10 minutes, by which time the chicken should be fully cooked.

10. Remove from the oven, stir and leave to rest for about 10 minutes. Then spoon off all excess ghee and reserve for another time.

11. Garnish with the garam masala, almonds, onion tarka and fresh coriander leaves.

NOTE
Steps 4 and 5 can be reduced in time to less than a minute, if you use the pre-made tarkas described on pages 31 and 32.

OPPOSITE PREVIOUS PAGE Clockwise from top: *Bhera Mansha Rezala* (creamy lamb curry, page 66), *Vegetable Biriani* (rice with sweet potato, green banana and parsnip, page 137) and *Bakhar Khani* (cheese-stuffed crispy layered paratha, page 147)

OPPOSITE Clockwise from top: *Motor Shuti Charchori* (dry cooked green split peas, page 129), *Hansha Tindaloo* (very hot duck curry, page 86) and *Moghul Paratha* (layered crispy bread, page 146). Scattered around are nagur chillies at various stages of ripeness

Morog Mosamman
STUFFED WHOLE CHICKEN

•

THIS is a Moslem dish that originated in ancient Persia. Peacock would have been the subject in those days, indeed until quite recently, and the dish would have been served on festive occasions. Nowadays a chicken or duck is used. I use a whole roasting chicken, with bones, but you can use a boned chicken for dramatic effect.

This dish is also known as *morgh* or *murgh kurzi* or *khazi* at our curry houses where, because of its specialist preparation and marination, you are requested to order it 24 hours in advance. At home you can extend the marination time for better penetration.

Try this dish as a Sunday lunch or Easter/Boxing Day alternative, and serve it as you would the Sunday roast – with all the trimmings.

NOTE
As the cavity size will vary from bird to bird, so must the exact amount of stuffing. A way around this is to bulk it up with chunks of raw potato, carrot, onion and/or garlic. Or you can add cooked rice and frozen peas if required.

———— SERVES 4–6 ————

1 roasting chicken, about 4 lb (1.8 kg)

MARINADE
12 garlic cloves, chopped
4–6 red cayenne chillies
2 tablespoons chopped red bell pepper
2 teaspoons chilli powder
2 teaspoons paprika
1 teaspoon Bangladeshi Garam Masala (see page 34)

2 tablespoons freshly squeezed lime juice
1 tablespoon red wine vinegar
1 tablespoon brown sugar
2 teaspoons salt
6 fl oz (175 ml) home-made yoghurt (see page 33)

STUFFING
12 quail eggs
stuffing (see pages 40, 42 or 46)

1. Mulch the marinade ingredients down in the food processor, using water if or as required, to create a thickish but pourable paste, and put in a large, non-metallic bowl.

2. Skin the chicken, wash it inside and out and remove unwanted items – the gizzard, giblets, etc. Dry it and slash the flesh with a sharp pointed knife.

3. Put the chicken into the bowl and massage the marinade into every part of it, inside and out. Cover the bowl with cling film and put it into the fridge for 24–60 hours (see page 17).

4. Pre-heat the oven to 375°F/190°C/Gas Mark 5.

5. Hardboil the quail eggs (4 minutes only in boiling water).

6. Make the stuffing, using any of the three stuffing recipes on pages 40, 42 or 46.

7. Shell the eggs and mix them, whole, into the stuffing. Cram the stuffing into the chicken, then coat the bird with excess marinade.

8. Carefully wrap the chicken in foil and place it on a rack above an oven tray in the oven.

9. Roast for a total of $1\frac{1}{2}$ hours for a 4 lb (1.8 kg) chicken. Deduct or add 4 minutes per $\frac{1}{4}$ lb (110 g) for weight under or over 4 lb (1.8 kg).

10. After 30 minutes of roasting remove the foil and baste the chicken with curry juices from the pan.

11. Repeat twice more, at 20 minute intervals.

12. When you have roasted the chicken for the allotted full time, check that it is cooked by removing the foil over a leg area. Poke a small knife blade into the flesh and if the liquid runs out clear, the chicken is ready. If the juices are pink, continue cooking in the oven for a few minutes more.

Hansha Tindaloo

VERY HOT DUCK CURRY

•

RASHEED'S wife, Roosha, laid on a very excellent lunch for us in their Sylhetti home. The meal was exquisite in every respect, and I was thrilled to find an abundance of fresh green chillies in many of the dishes. Rasheed confessed to being a chilli minimalist, but Roosha, once she realised I was a chilliholic, trilled with glee. She had found a chilli ally in the unlikeliest guest – an Englishman!

'You like hot? We call it Tindaloo.' She disappeared into the kitchen, returning with a bright red, fresh, irregularly shaped chilli. 'Try this,' she said, 'but be careful.'

As I nibbled the top off, the family screamed in horror. Joy – incendiary joy. It was a Habanero/Scotch Bonnet type, at level 9 or 10 on the heat scale. In all my trips to the subcontinent I had never found this heat level before. It was blissful and, being used to such delights at home, I nibbled the whole thing down. The family watched wide-eyed, Roosha the more so. 'You are a strong man,' she marvelled. And she has probably dined out on the story ever since. The particular red chilli is called the Nagur and comes from that town in India.

Tindaloo means extremely hot in Bengali. At the British curry restaurant, the word became confused with *Vindaloo*. Pronounced vin-*dar*-loo, with the emphasis on the second syllable, this is a Goan pork and chilli curry. Bangladeshi **T**indaloo, emphasis on the first syllable, is the country's hottest dish.

Here it is, made with duck and Habaneros or Scotch Bonnets. If you can't get these chillies, use red cayennes (which are heat scale 8) but increase the quantities.

—— SERVES 4 ——

1½ lb (675 g) duck breasts, weighed after removing all skin and fat
10 tablespoons butter ghee
6–8 garlic cloves, very finely chopped
8 oz (225 g) onions, very finely chopped
2–4 red Habanero/Scotch Bonnet/Nagur chillies, chopped
up to 8 fl oz (250 ml) akhni stock (see page 38) or water
2 tablespoons chopped fresh coriander leaves
salt to taste

SPICES
2 teaspoons ground coriander
1 teaspoon ground cummin
1 teaspoon Bangladeshi Garam Masala (see page 34)
1 teaspoon turmeric
1–3 teaspoons extra-hot chilli powder

GARNISH
Bangladeshi Garam Masala (see page 34)
toasted almonds
Onion Tarka (see page 31)
fresh coriander leaves

1. Cut the duck into suitable sized cubes and pre-heat the oven to 375°F/190°C/Gas Mark 5.

2. Heat the ghee on the stove in a 4–5 pint (2.25–2.75 litre) flameproof casserole dish with a lid.

3. Add the **spices** and stir-fry for 30 seconds. Add the garlic, lower the heat and obtain a golden brown tarka (see note) over about 5 minutes.

4. Add the onions and continue stir-frying on a low heat (just sizzling) to continue the tarka, taking around 15 minutes.

5. Add the duck and chillies and continue to stir-fry for about 10 minutes, 'sealing' the meat.

6. Put the lidded casserole into the oven.

7. After 20 minutes, inspect and stir. The duck should not be shrivelling or drying out. We want it to be juicy, in a juicy gravy. Add just enough akhni stock or water to ensure this, now and throughout the remaining cooking, as needed.

8. Inspect again after 20 minutes. Add the chopped coriander leaves and salt to taste. Return to the oven for a final 10 minutes, by which time the duck should be really tender. (If it isn't quite tender, give it a little more oven time.)

9. Remove from the oven, stir and leave to rest for about 10 minutes. Then spoon off all excess ghee and reserve for another time.

10. Garnish with the garam masala, almonds, onion tarka and fresh coriander leaves.

NOTE
Steps 3 and 4 can be reduced in time to less than a minute, if you use the pre-made tarkas described on pages 31 and 32.

Anday Dopeyaja
EGG AND ONION CURRY
•

THERE is an antiquarian book that describes court life under the emperor Akbar. Called the *Ain-i-Akbari*, it was written in Persia by the historian Abdul Fazl in 1590. It includes plentiful information about court dishes; and tells us that the Moghul emperors greatly enjoyed their food which was developed to great heights during their reigns. It was the emperors' custom to abstain from meat from time to time. Eggs, however, were acceptable and this dish, *dopeyaja* (or *dopiaza*), was originally a meat dish cooked with ghee, spices, yoghurt and a lot of onion. *Do* means two and *peyaja* (or *piaza*) is onion. *Anday* or *dim* means egg.

Dopeyaja, with any main ingredient, became very popular in Bengal probably because, one, the Bengalis love onion and, two, they adore its sweet taste. Here, then, is Akbar's favourite dish. I have used bantam eggs because their small size is attractive, and they are not uncommon in Bangladesh. Serve with a couple of other curries and rice.

—— SERVES 4 ——

8–12 bantam eggs or small hen eggs
4 tablespoons mustard blend oil
4–6 garlic cloves, very finely chopped
1 inch (2.5 cm) piece fresh ginger, very finely chopped
8 oz (225 g) red onions, chopped
2 fresh red chillies, sliced
1 tablespoon chopped red bell pepper
4 tablespoons chopped spring onion leaves
4–6 cherry tomatoes, halved
6 tablespoons home-made yoghurt (see page 33)
2 teaspoons Bangladeshi Garam Masala (see page 34)
1 tablespoon brown sugar

1 tablespoon chopped fresh coriander leaves
3–4 fresh mint leaves, chopped
salt to taste

SPICES
$\frac{1}{3}$ teaspoon turmeric
$1\frac{1}{2}$ teaspoons ground coriander
1 teaspoon ground cummin
1 teaspoon paprika
$\frac{1}{2}$ teaspoon ground cinnamon
$\frac{1}{2}$ teaspoon ground cardamom
$\frac{1}{4}$ teaspoon asafoetida

GARNISH
Onion Tarka (see page 31)

1. Hardboil the bantam eggs by placing them in boiling water and boiling for 12 minutes. Cool them enough to remove the shells.

2. During this, heat the oil in a karahi or wok and stir-fry the **spices** for a minute. Add the garlic and ginger and stir-fry for 30 seconds then add the onions. Lower the heat and gently simmer the onions to a tarka, over about 15 minutes (see note).

3. Add the chillies, pepper, spring onion leaves and tomatoes and stir-fry on a slightly higher heat for 5 minutes.

4. Add the yoghurt and, when simmering, add the eggs, garam masala, sugar and chopped coriander and mint leaves.

5. Simmer for 3–4 minutes more, then add salt to taste. Garnish with the onion tarka.

NOTE
Step 2 can be reduced in time to less than a minute, if you use the pre-made tarka described on page 31.

—— *Variation* ——

Add eight cooked potatoes (bantam egg size) at Step 3, for a more substantial curry.

CHAPTER 5

❖◈❖

FISH

BANGLADESHIS are not vegetarian by choice but, as we have seen on pages 56 and 75, meat and poultry are scarce so they are confirmed eaters of fish and this provides about 75 per cent of their protein. With so much natural water, hundreds of freshwater species thrive, taking advantage of the annual floods to breed 'on land', so to speak, which makes them available to farmers. In fact, 60 per cent of all households fish, and fish markets in every town and village in Bangladesh display an amazing range of shapes and sizes, all so fresh (many are still alive) that they would put our best supermarkets to shame.

The most popular fish are *rui* (or *rhui*) – their king of fish – a kind of large, meaty, pink-fleshed carp; *bekti*, which is larger and white fleshed with minimal bones; the bony *hilsa*, a type of herring; *katla*, a smaller carp; *pomfret*, a small, plump, flattish fish; and *magur*, a catfish.

These species are increasingly available in the West, frozen and even fresh, and are worth trying to get. But I have given substitutes in the recipes which follow.

Bangladesh has realised that it has a great potential as a fish and shellfish exporter (already 12 per cent of its gross national product is in this area) and new freezing factories are coming on stream all the time. Consequently, more 'exotic' fish are becoming available in the West. Species which you are increasingly likely to see include *aieer*, *bhing*, *boaal* (like whiting), *gojar*, *koi*, *pabla*, *pangas*, *puti* and *shol*. Try them if you can.

Bangladeshi shellfish are world class. The celebrated Bengal tiger or jumbo prawn leads the pack for size. It grows up to 12 inches (30.5 cm) in length and many are farmed at Chittagong. Other prawns, of all sizes, are popular and five recipes cover the topic. And, of course, I could not miss out lobster.

Bangladesh is a master of resources and a visit to any market will reveal literally dozens of types of dried fish of all sizes and colours. Though quite salty, these can be reconstituted in water (or deep-fried) and supply Bangladeshis with fish during the annual droughts. India's Bombay duck is a dried fish and available in Asian stores, as are some other species. I have not given specific recipes for dried fish (*shukna* or *shukki maach*) here, but my favourite way of cooking them is to deep-fry them until they are crisp and eat them with aperitifs.

Nothing goes to waste in Bangladesh but I have omitted one recipe because we Westerners are so squeamish: *ghonto* (fish head) curry. However, I have given an exotic recipe for the daring: eel curry!

Golda Chingri Jal

KING PRAWN STIR-FRY

•

GOLDA are large king prawns. To be precise, you get between six and eight to the pound, and when you tell that to your fishmonger he will know exactly what you mean. They are prolific in the Bay of Bengal, as are all prawns. This stir-fry produces quick, tasty results.

———— SERVES 4 ————

4 tablespoons butter ghee
2 teaspoons Panch Foran (see page 40)
½ teaspoon turmeric
6 garlic cloves, chopped
1 inch (2.5 cm) piece fresh ginger, chopped
8 oz (225 g) onions, sliced

1½ lb (675 g) large king prawns (about 10–12 prawns), peeled and de-veined
2 tablespoons chopped red bell pepper
1 tablespoon tomato ketchup
2–4 fresh green chillies, sliced
1 tablespoon fresh coriander leaves
salt to taste

1. Heat the ghee in a karahi or wok and stir-fry the panch foran and turmeric for 30 seconds. Add the garlic and continue to stir-fry for 30 seconds, then add the ginger and stir-fry for 30 seconds more.

2. Add the onions and stir-fry for at least 5 minutes.

3. Add the prawns and stir-fry for about 5 minutes. Add water, a spoonful at a time, as needed.

4. Add the remaining ingredients and simmer/stir-fry for 8–10 minutes more.

Sorrisa Jumbo Chingri

MUSTARD JUMBO PRAWNS

•

I DIDN'T meet any elephants in Bangladesh, though I'm told that plenty live and work in the south, and there is said to be one resident jumbo in Sylhet. But I did meet many a native jumbo prawn. They grow to a vast 12 inches (30.5 cm). When you see them swimming in tanks their full size is quite surprising and you can see why the natives call them jumbo prawns. Equally surprising is their natural silver-grey colour which contrasts with black stripes, giving rise to their other name – tiger prawns. The pinkness comes about with the application of heat.

Mustard is *shorse/sorsi* in Bangladeshi and this method involves making a paste, then wrapping the prawns (in a banana leaf over there – foil over here) and steaming them.

———— SERVES 4 ————

4 Bengali jumbo prawns, each weighing 4 oz (110 g) or more

PASTE
6 tablespoons mustard blend oil
2 tablespoons black mustard seeds
1 teaspoon yellow mustard powder
1 teaspoon turmeric

2 tablespoons chopped fresh coriander leaves
3–4 fresh green cayenne chillies, chopped
2 tablespoons coconut milk powder
½ teaspoon salt

GARNISH
salt
Cox's Bazaar Hot Sprinkler (see page 37)

1. Shell the prawns but leave the tail on if you like. Remove the vein down the back using a sharp paring knife. Wash the prawns and pat them dry.

2. Mulch down the paste ingredients in the food processor to obtain a thick spreadable paste, using the bare minimum of water.

3. Spread the paste on each prawn, then carefully and loosely wrap each in kitchen foil.

4. Using a steamer, boil a quantity of water in the lower compartment. If you do not have a steamer use a sieve standing clear of the water. Put the lid on.

5. Steam the prawns for 15 minutes (ensuring that the water does not run out).

6. Garnish with the salt and hot sprinkler.

Bagda Chingri Korma

MILDLY CURRIED SMALL KING PRAWNS

•

BAGDA (king prawns) are about half the size of the *goldas* in the recipe on page 91. They average between 12 and 15 to the pound and, again, are prolific in Bangladesh, being fished in the Bay of Bengal and along the 120 kilometres of beaches in the south of the country.

This splendid korma recipe hails from the southerly town of Cox's Bazaar, where you will find the excellent Sagorika Seafood restaurant on the seafront. The town got its bizarre name in 1798 when the East India Company sent one Captain Cox to establish an outpost in the area.

——— SERVES 4 ———

4 tablespoons sunflower oil
1 teaspoon turmeric
2 teaspoons chilli powder
6 garlic cloves, very finely chopped
6 oz (175 g) onions, very finely chopped
1½ lb (675 g) king prawns (about 18–22 prawns), peeled and de-veined
2–4 fresh green chillies, sliced
2 teaspoons Bangladeshi Garam Masala (see page 34)

6–10 fresh or dried curry leaves
6 cherry tomatoes, quartered
5 fl oz (150 ml) single cream
4 tablespoons coconut milk powder
2 tablespoons chopped fresh coriander leaves
salt to taste
Cox's Bazaar Hot Sprinkler (see page 37) to garnish

1. Heat the oil in a karahi or wok. Stir-fry the turmeric, chilli powder and garlic for 30 seconds. Add the onions and stir-fry for 5 minutes or more.

2. Add the prawns, chilli, garam masala, curry leaves and tomatoes and stir-fry for 5 minutes.

3. Add the cream and coconut milk powder, and stir-fry for 5 more minutes.

4. Add the chopped coriander leaves and salt to taste. Stir-fry for up to 5 more minutes, garnish with the hot sprinkler and serve.

Chota Chingri Chittagong
TINY SHRIMP CURRY

•

THIS recipe uses tiny thumbnail shrimps, the smallest (*chota*) you can buy. These have shells so soft that you don't need to peel them. Eat them shells, legs, heads, tails and all.

The secret of making them palatable is to fry them first, then use this recipe from the hilly Chittagong district in the south of Bangladesh. A fishing town, built on the seaside 2,000 years ago, Chittagong got its name when its Buddhist inhabitants beat off the first Moslem invaders in the twelfth century. A monument was erected with an inscription reading *Tse-Tse-Gong* – more or less 'peace not war' – hence the town's name.

Chittagong is now a vast commercial port and fishing centre, where the aptly named Curry House restaurant at the Hotel Hawaii gets the local thumbs-up for dishes like this one.

NOTE

You can use dried curry leaves if fresh ones are unobtainable. But add them at Step 5.

——— SERVES 4 ———

6–8 garlic cloves, chopped
15–20 fresh curry leaves
1 tablespoon brown sugar
3 tablespoons sunflower oil
1½ lb (675 g) tiny shrimps with shells on
4 tablespoons coconut milk powder
3–4 fresh red cayenne chillies, cut into small rings
salt to taste
lime wedges to serve

SPICES

2 teaspoons black mustard seeds
2 teaspoons white poppy seeds
½ teaspoon black cummin seeds
1 teaspoon dry red chilli seeds
3 tablespoons desiccated coconut
½ teaspoon turmeric

GARNISH

Cox's Bazaar Hot Sprinkler (see page 37)
crispy Onion Tarka (see page 31)

1. Dry roast the **spices** (see page 25) then grind them in a mortar and pestle or spice mill with the garlic, fresh curry leaves, sugar and enough water to make a pourable paste. (You could also use a blender.)

2. Heat the oil in a karahi or wok. Stir-fry the shrimps for about 5 minutes. Remove them from the oil and set aside.

3. Ensuring the oil is still hot, stir-fry the paste for a couple of minutes.

4. Add a couple of spoons of water to loosen the frying paste, then add the shrimps.

5. Stir-fry for 5 minutes more, loosening with water as needed.

6. Add the coconut milk powder, chillies and enough water to make a rich-looking gravy. Stir-fry for 3 minutes more. Salt to taste.

7. Serve with lime wedges and garnish with the hot sprinkler and onion tarka.

Puishak Chingri
SHRIMP CURRY WITH GREEN LEAVES
•

A VERY simple variation on the previous recipe. Jute, which comes from the bark of a leafy plant and is used to make sacking and carpet backing, is one of Bangladesh's main exports. In the age-old tradition of 'waste not, want not' young, tender jute leaves (called *patsag* in Bengali, *patua-sag* in Hindi/Urdu and *puishak* in Bangladeshi) are used to create a vegetable dish.

The leaves can occasionally be obtained from Asian greengrocers. Alternatively, use very young, tender spinach leaves mixed with basil and rocket.

NOTE
You can cut back the shrimp quantity if you wish.

———— SERVES 4 ————

In addition to the ingredients opposite you will need:
1 lb (450 g) puishak or 12 oz (350 g) young spinach

2 oz (50 g) basil leaves
2 oz (50 g) rocket leaves

1. Wash and chop the puishak or spinach leaves, the basil and the rocket.

2. Follow the opposite recipe, adding the leaves at stage 6. Continue with the above recipe.

Rhui Cutlet

BATTER-COATED PINK FISH

•

Rhui (or *rahu*) is a large, freshwater fish, regarded by Bangladeshis as their 'king of the river'. It is a type of golden carp, with pink flesh, and grows to between 2 and 10 kilograms. If you cannot get carp, substitute trout or salmon. Any of these are particularly good for this dish.

The fish is cut crossways across its centre to form four oval steaks about 1½ inches (3.75 cm) thick, then dipped in Bengal gram flour (*besan*) and fried to a crispy cutlet, which is garnished with a special *tarka*. This recipe takes pride of place at the sumptuous Sonargaon hotel.

Serve with a wet curry or two and rice, or, with Bangladeshi Garnish (see page 150), lemon wedges and chutneys for a starter.

———— SERVES 4 ————

4 fish 'steaks', cut on the bone (see above)
oil for deep-frying

TARKA
4 tablespoons mustard blend oil
2 teaspoons black mustard seeds
½ teaspoon turmeric
4 garlic cloves, sliced
1 inch (2.5 cm) piece fresh ginger, very finely chopped

8 oz (225 g) onions, sliced
3–4 dry red chillies, chopped

BATTER
4 oz (110 g) gram flour (besan)
1 tablespoon bottled curry paste
2 tablespoons lemon or lime juice
1 teaspoon chilli powder
1 teaspoon salt

1. Start the tarka first and let it sizzle whilst the remainder of the recipe cooks. Heat the oil in a flat frying pan. Stir-fry the seeds and turmeric for 30 seconds. Add the garlic and ginger and stir-fry for 30 seconds more. Lower the heat, add the onions and chillies and stir-fry at the sizzle for at least 15 minutes until golden and crispy (see note).

2. Wash and dry the fish steaks.

3. Make the batter by mixing the ingredients with enough water to make a stiffish paste, which will drop sluggishly off the spoon. Let it stand for at least 10 minutes, during which time the mixture will absorb the moisture.

4. Meanwhile, heat the deep-frying oil to 375°F/190°C. This temperature is below smoking point and will cause a sliver of batter to splutter a bit, then float more or less at once.

5. Inspect the mixture. There must be no batter 'powder' left. It must be well mixed.

6. Coat the fish steaks with the batter.

7. Carefully lower one fish steak into the oil. Place the others in, allowing about 20 seconds between each to maintain oil temperature.

8. Deep-fry for 10–12 minutes, turning a few times. Remove the fish from the oil, drain well on kitchen paper and pour the tarka over them.

NOTE
Step 1 can be reduced in time to less than a minute, if you use the pre-made tarkas described on pages 31 and 32.

Bayam Teknaf

EEL CURRY

•

BANGLADESH shares a small part of its southern border with Burma, in the form of the river Naff and, prior to 1947, before the British withdrew, one could cross it over a bridge near the town of Teknaf. This has not been possible since then, and the border road has long since returned to being impenetrable jungle. Eels, colourfully called the 'snake fish' (*bayam*), know no boundaries and abound in the river Naff, as they do elsewhere in Bangladesh. Recipes are equally abundant. For those who enjoy things exotic here is an authentic eel curry, using the interesting *dana-zira* spice mixture.

Serve with a vegetable or lentil curry and a bread or rice.

—— SERVES 4 ——

1 eel, weighing about 2 lb 3 oz (1 kg)
$\frac{1}{4}$ pint (150 ml) vinegar, any type
3 tablespoons salt
6 tablespoons mustard blend oil
2 teaspoons black mustard seeds
3 teaspoons very finely chopped garlic cloves
8 oz (225 g) onions, very finely chopped
1 tablespoon brown sugar or molasses
3–4 fresh green chillies, sliced
14 fl oz (400 ml) akhni stock (see page 38) or water
2–3 bay leaves
1 × 2 inch (5 cm) piece cassia bark

2 teaspoons Bangladeshi Garam Masala (see page 34)
salt to taste

SPICES (dana-zira)
1 tablespoon coriander seeds, roasted and ground
2 teaspoons white cummin seeds, roasted and ground
1 teaspoon yellow mustard powder
1–2 teaspoons chopped dried red chillies
$\frac{1}{2}$ teaspoon asafoetida

1. Get the fishmonger to behead, de-fin/tail and gut the eel and cut it into segments.

2. Soak the eel in a large non-metallic bowl containing 1 pint (600 ml) water, the vinegar and salt for 2 hours. Drain the eel and rinse it in clean water.

3. Heat the oil and stir-fry the mustard seeds for 10 seconds. Add the **spices** and continue to stir-fry for a minute.

4. Add the garlic and onions and stir-fry for at least 10 minutes.

5. Add the eel, sugar or molasses and the chillies and stir-fry for 2–3 minutes.

6. Add the akhni stock or water, bay leaves and cassia bark and simmer for 30 minutes, stirring from time to time. Add the garam masala and salt to taste.

Magur Kalia

CATFISH CURRY

•

CATFISH is readily available in the West. A good freshwater species is channel catfish. Two varieties, the larger *magur* and the smaller *shing*, are also readily available in Bangladesh.

The whiskers are a bit off-putting (so get the fishmonger to skin, fillet and gut the fish for you) but the flesh is fine, especially when curried in the Bangladeshi *kalia* method, using red ingredients. We met meat kalia on page 61, cooked in a casserole. This is karahi-cooked and takes considerably less time – and it's delicious. Be brave – try it!

──── SERVES 4 ────

1½ lb (675 g) catfish, weighed after removing all unwanted matter
4 tablespoons sunflower oil
2 garlic cloves, chopped
8 oz (225 g) onions, finely sliced
1 teaspoon chopped dry red chilli
1–2 fresh red chillies, sliced
2 teaspoons tomato purée
1 tablespoon brown sugar
2 tablespoons chopped red bell pepper
2 teaspoons Bangladeshi Garam Masala (see page 34)

1 tablespoon finely chopped fresh coriander leaves
salt to taste

SPICES

1 teaspoon white cummin seeds
½ teaspoon coriander seeds, crushed
2–3 bay leaves
1 teaspoon white poppy seeds (posta dana)
½ teaspoon chilli powder
½ teaspoon turmeric

1. Cut the fish into bite-sized pieces.

2. Heat the oil in a karahi or wok. Add the garlic and stir-fry for 30 seconds. Add the **spices** and stir-fry for 30 seconds more. Add the onions and, lowering the heat, fry until they become a tarka (see page 31), adding splashes of water, if needed, to prevent sticking.

3. Add the fish pieces and stir-fry for 5 minutes.

4. Add the dry and fresh chillies, tomato purée, sugar, pepper and a little water and stir-fry for 10 minutes or so.

5. Add the garam masala, chopped coriander leaves and salt to taste. Simmer for up to 5 minutes more then serve.

Bekti Tandoori

FISH TANDOORI

•

BEKTI is a very large river fish with white, minimally bony flesh, which abounds in Bangladesh. We do not have a comparable freshwater species – river shad comes closest – but any steak-like fish will do for this recipe. Cod or haddock is fine. But try your fishmonger. Frozen, even fresh, bekti is available in the West at times.

Serve with rice and a vegetable curry.

NOTE

This can be a suitable starter. Halve all quantities, but follow the recipe exactly. Serve with Bangladeshi Garnish (see page 150).

———— SERVES 4 ————

8 oz (225 g) onions, roughly chopped
10 garlic cloves, roughly chopped
4–6 red chillies, roughly chopped
1 inch (2.5 cm) piece fresh ginger, roughly chopped
3 fl oz (75 ml) home-made yoghurt (see page 33)
2 tablespoons freshly squeezed lime juice
1 tablespoon white wine vinegar
$1\frac{1}{2}$ teaspoons salt
$1\frac{1}{2}$ lb (675 g) bekti or white fish, filleted, skinned and cut into approx. $2\times1\times\frac{1}{2}$ inch ($5\times2.5\times1.25$ cm) slices

2–3 tablespoons butter ghee
chopped chives or fresh coriander leaves to garnish

SPICES

2 teaspoons chilli powder
2 teaspoons paprika
1 teaspoon ground coriander
1 teaspoon Bangladeshi Garam Masala (see page 34)
$\frac{1}{2}$ teaspoon mango powder

1. Put the onions, garlic, red chillies, ginger and enough water to achieve a runny consistency into a food processor (in batches) and pulse to a runny mush. Strain this mush to obtain all the liquid you can. Discard the solids.

2. Put this liquid into a large, non-metallic bowl along with the yoghurt, lime juice, vinegar, salt and **spices** and beat with a fork to mix it into the marinade.

3. Add the fish slices, coating them with the marinade. Cover the bowl with cling film and put into the fridge for up to 3 hours.

4. Pre-heat the grill to medium. Line the grill pan rack with foil, put the fish slices on it and place the pan at the midway position.

5. Remove after 5 minutes and turn the fish over. Baste with excess marinade. Grill for 3 minutes more.

6. Turn the fish pieces over again and brush with ghee. Grill at the highest position for a minute to singe (but not burn) the fish.

7. Serve garnished with chopped chives or coriander.

Hilsa Maachhi Vhaji Jol

FISH AND VEGETABLE CURRY

•

HILSA is a very bony, freshwater ('sweet water' in Bangladesh) fish which is commonly found all over the country, especially in the south. Bangladeshis adore chewing its multitude of thin, needle-like bones, though this may appeal less to Westerners, who prefer fillets or, at worst, large bones. Hilsa is a member of the herring family and herrings, though seafish, can be substituted for it. Perch would also be fine.

The *jol* or *jhol* process (not to be confused with *jal* or *jhal*, see next recipe) means literally to cook (fish and vegetables) in ample water.

As with most curries, the initial ingredients are fried then stewed in water. The result should be quite runny, though this will depend on how much water you choose to use.

In this jol I have specified the authentic vegetables for this dish – *potol* (gourd), green banana and aubergine. Marrow or courgettes could be substituted for the *potol*. Serve with rice.

———— SERVES 4 ————

1 lb (450 g) hilsa, herring or perch, weighed after Step 1
6 tablespoons mustard blend oil
1 teaspoon chopped dry red chillies
1 teaspoon Panch Foran (see page 36)
1 green cooking banana (plantain), skinned and chopped
8 baby new potatoes, halved
1 potol/parwal gourd or courgette/marrow, chopped
1 small aubergine, chopped
salt to taste
fresh coriander leaves to garnish

PURÉE

½ teaspoon turmeric
1 teaspoon ground cummin
1 teaspoon ground coriander
½ teaspoon ground black pepper
3 oz (75 g) onion, chopped
1 tablespoon tomato purée

PASTE

1 teaspoon turmeric
1 teaspoon salt
4 tablespoons gram flour (besan)
1 tablespoon vinegar

1. Make a pourable paste of the paste ingredients, using a little water. Remove the head, fins and tail of the fish and gut it.

2. Chop the fish into bite-sized chunks. Wash the chunks, dry them and coat them in the paste. Set them aside for an hour.

3. Grind the purée ingredients together using a little water to achieve a thickish purée.

4. Heat the oil in a 4 pint (2.25 litre) lidded saucepan. Stir-fry the chillies and panch foran for 30 seconds. Stir-fry the purée for a couple of minutes. Add the fish chunks, and stir-fry these for about 3 minutes.

5. Remove the fish pieces and set aside. Add the banana and potatoes and stir-fry for a further 2 minutes.

6. Add 1 pint (600 ml) water to the saucepan and bring to the simmer. Put the lid on and simmer for about 10–15 minutes.

7. Add the fish chunks, gourd and aubergine and continue simmering with the lid on, stirring occasionally while the water reduces a little for a further 10 minutes. Add salt to taste.

8. Garnish with the fresh coriander leaves.

Katla Jal

FRIED FISH CURRY

•

$\mathbf{W}$E HAVE met the *jal* or frying process in several recipes (see index). Not to be confused with the *jhol* (boiling) process in the previous recipe, it requires virtually no water. *Katla*, like *rhui* which we met on page 96, is another member of the carp family, only it is smaller, a little oilier – which makes it a good candidate for stir-frying – and silver rather than golden. Pilchards or the smaller sardines (young pilchards) are suitable substitutes. Buy them ready filleted.

—— SERVES 4 ——

4 × 8–10 oz (225–300 g) katla or pilchards or
   8 × 4–5 oz (110–150 g) sardines
4 tablespoons sunflower oil
1 teaspoon black mustard seeds
1 teaspoon yellow mustard seeds
1 teaspoon black cummin seeds
4–6 garlic cloves, chopped
4–6 spring onions, bulbs and leaves, chopped
2–3 dry red chillies, chopped
lime wedges to serve

PASTE
½ teaspoon turmeric
1 teaspoon chilli powder
4 tablespoons gram flour (besan)
1 tablespoon vinegar

GARNISH
Cox's Bazaar Hot Sprinkler (see page 37)
salt to taste

1. Mix the paste ingredients together, using just enough water to achieve a thick paste.

2. Keep the fish whole, but behead them if you prefer. Wash and dry them. Coat the fish with the paste.

3. Heat the oil in a large, flat frying pan. Stir-fry the seeds for 30 seconds. Add the garlic and stir-fry for 30 seconds more. Add the spring onions and chillies and stir-fry the mixture for about 5 minutes.

4. Lower the heat and add the fish. Fry for 5–6 minutes, adding splashes of water to prevent sticking.

5. Turn the fish over and continue for 5–6 minutes more, frying and watering, but essentially keeping the fish dry and crispy.

6. Raise the heat to achieve ultimate crispness. Sprinkle with hot sprinkler and salt, and serve with lime wedges.

Dohi Boal Maach

FISH COOKED IN YOGHURT

•

B_{OAL} is a rather ugly, long, thin, round white fish with 'whiskers'. The white-fleshed pomfret can be used here. Popular on the subcontinent and prolific in the Bay of Bengal, pomfret is also caught by Spanish and Portuguese fishermen, so it is available fresh in all European markets.

In this typical Bangladeshi recipe, yoghurt (*dohi*) creates a sour taste and creamy texture. Serve with plain rice.

———— SERVES 4 ————

4 tablespoons freshly squeezed lime juice

1 teaspoon chilli powder

4 small or 2 large boal or pomfret, total weight $1\frac{1}{4}$ lb (500 g) after Step 1

2 tablespoons mustard blend oil

$\frac{1}{2}$ teaspoon red chilli seeds

$\frac{1}{2}$ teaspoon wild onion seeds

$\frac{1}{2}$ teaspoon white cummin seeds

2–4 tablespoons sunflower oil

5 fl oz (150 ml) home-made yoghurt (see page 33)

2–3 fresh red chillies, cut into rings

salt to taste

PURÉE

1 teaspoon turmeric

6 garlic cloves

1 inch (2.5 cm) piece fresh ginger

2–4 fresh green chillies

1 teaspoon yellow mustard

1 tablespoon vinegar, any type

1. Mix the lime juice with the chilli powder. Gut, fin and behead the fish.

2. Cut the fish into cross-sections, then wash them inside and out. Dry them and put them in a non-metallic bowl and add the lime juice/chilli mixture. Cover the bowl and let it stand for 1 hour or so.

3. Grind the purée ingredients into a pourable purée, using water as required.

4. Heat the oil in a 4 pint (2.25 litre) saucepan. Stir-fry the seeds for 30 seconds. Add the purée and continue stir-frying for a minute or so, until the oil separates. Remove from the heat.

5. In a flat frying pan, heat the sunflower oil and briskly stir-fry the fish pieces for about 5 minutes to brown them.

6. Return the saucepan and its mixture to the heat. When sizzling, transfer the fish and juices to the saucepan. Stir well, then add the yoghurt.

7. Gently simmer for 10 minutes, stirring from time to time. Add the fresh red chillies and salt to taste and simmer for 2–3 minutes.

Maach Koftas

FISH BALLS

•

KOFTAS, or small fried balls, can be made of meat, vegetable or fish. Any large fleshy fish will do. Bangladeshis would use *rhui*, *bekti* or *katla*, all of which we met earlier, or two large fish we have not met: *foli* or *chitol*. Having said that, two highly satisfactory and readily available fish for koftas are cod steaks for white koftas, or salmon for pink ones.

The resultant deep-fried batter coated balls make splendid canapés or starters. Alternatively, they can be served in a curry gravy (see opposite).

——— MAKES 8 large or 16 small koftas ———

semolina or cornflour

oil for deep-frying

2 tablespoons chopped fresh red chilli

2 teaspoons Panch Foran (see page 36)

FISH MIXTURE

1 lb (450 g) cod or salmon skinless fillet

$\frac{1}{2}$ lb (225 g) mashed potato

2–3 large spring onions, leaves and bulbs, chopped

1 tablespoon chopped fresh coriander leaves

BATTER

4 oz (110 g) gram flour (besan)

1 tablespoon bottled curry paste (see page 26)

$\frac{1}{2}$ teaspoon salt

1. Mix the fish ingredients together in a food processor to achieve a mouldable mixture.

2. Mix the batter ingredients with just enough water to achieve a pourable batter.

3. Divide the fish mixture into eight for larger koftas or 12 or 16 for smaller ones.

4. Sprinkle semolina or cornflour on the work top. Roll the koftas on the top to achieve balls.

5. Pre-heat the oil for deep-frying to 375°F/190°C (chip-frying temperature).

6. Immerse the koftas in the batter mix, then lower them, one at a time, into the hot oil allowing some seconds between each one to maintain oil temperature.

7. Deep-fry for about 8–10 minutes, after which the koftas will be golden and cooked. Remove and rest on kitchen paper.

8. Serve hot or cold, or add hot to the curry gravy in the following recipe.

Maach Kofta Curry

FISH BALL CURRY

•

MAKE 8 or 16 fish *koftas* as described in the previous recipe. Make the following gravy in advance. Add the hot deep-fried *koftas* to the hot cooked gravy and serve with a vegetable and/or lentil dish and rice.

———— SERVES 4 ————

8 or 16 koftas (see opposite)

KOFTA GRAVY
4 tablespoons butter ghee
½ teaspoon black cummin seeds
½ teaspoon lovage seeds (ajwain)
½ teaspoon white sesame seeds
4–6 garlic cloves, very finely chopped
8 oz (225 g) onions, very finely chopped
14 oz (400 g) tinned tomatoes, chopped
2–4 fresh green chillies, sliced
10–12 fresh or dried curry leaves

1 tablespoon chopped fresh coriander leaves
salt to taste

SPICES
1 teaspoon turmeric
2 teaspoons Bangladeshi Garam Masala (see page 34)
1 teaspoon chilli powder
¼ teaspoon asafoetida

1. Mix the **spices** with water, to make a pourable paste.

2. Heat the ghee in a karahi or wok. Stir-fry the seeds for 20 seconds. Add the garlic and stir-fry for 30 seconds more. Add the spice paste and stir-fry until the oil 'floats' – about 1½–2 minutes.

3. Add the onions and lower the heat. Stir-fry for 15–20 minutes to achieve a tarka (see note).

4. Add enough water to create a nice, rich gravy, with the tomatoes, chillies, curry leaves and chopped coriander leaves.

5. Simmer for about 10 minutes. Add any spare batter mix from step 6 of the previous recipe. Simmer on a while longer to allow the gravy to thicken a little. Salt to taste.

6. Add the hot koftas and serve.

NOTE
Step 3 can be reduced in time to less than a minute, if you use the pre-made tarka described on page 31.

Boro Chingri Korma

LOBSTER CURRY

•

Just as there must always be an exotic dish or two in any cookbook (see brain on page 72 and eel on page 98), by the same token there must be at least one luxury one. And this is it. Lobster cooked in creamy coconut milk is luxury indeed, although it should be said that lobsters breed prolifically in the warm balmy waters of the Bay of Bengal. Strictly speaking, they are spiny lobsters (or rock lobsters a.k.a. crawfish, but not crayfish, which are much smaller). European lobsters are larger than their Bengali counterparts and are identified by an enormous pair of pincers or claws. This is all a little academic, because it is easier to buy ready cooked and shelled pre-packed lobster meat (fresh or frozen) for this typical Bangladeshi curry restaurant creamy curry.

One more bit of dogma about lobster. If you have gone to all this expense already, hang it, go the whole hog and serve it with pink champagne! My Bangladeshi friends will forgive this indulgence, I'm sure – after all, if wine was good enough for the Emperor Akbar . . .

––––– SERVES 4 –––––

4 tablespoons butter ghee
4 garlic cloves, very finely chopped
8 oz (225 g) onions, very finely chopped
2–4 fresh red chillies, sliced
4 plum tomatoes, chopped
2 tablespoons chopped fresh mint
1 tablespoon chopped fresh coriander
  leaves
1½ lb (675 g) cooked lobster, cut into bite-
  sized pieces
20–30 saffron strands

14 fl oz (400 ml) tinned coconut milk
salt to taste

SPICES
1 teaspoon white cummin seeds
1 teaspoon bottled curry paste (see page 26)
2 teaspoons bottled red tandoori paste (see
  page 26)

GARNISH
crispy Onion Tarka (see page 31)
fresh coriander leaves

1. Heat the ghee in a karahi or wok and stir-fry the **spices** for 1 minute. Add the garlic and stir-fry for a minute more, then add the onions and stir-fry for at least 10 minutes until they are golden.

2. Add the chillies, tomatoes, mint and chopped coriander leaves and stir-fry for 3 minutes more.

3. Now add the lobster, saffron and coconut milk and simmer for 5 minutes. Add salt to taste. Garnish with onion tarka and fresh coriander leaves.

CHAPTER 6

❖

VEGETABLES

ANGLADESHIS adore their vegetables, and with good reason – there are so many good ones. All the established Western vegetables are there, of course: beans, cabbages, carrots, cauliflowers, peas, potatoes, pumpkins, spinach and tomatoes. Recipes including them are in this chapter.

The importation of exotic fruits and vegetables (known for decades as 'queer gear' at Covent Garden) improves all the time, and most of them – green bananas, aubergines, green mangos, okra, white radish and gourds – have been so readily available for so long that we take them for granted. Special Bangladeshi vegetables include two types of leaves loosely called spinach – *lal shak* and *puishak* – and gourds such as *chichinga* (snake gourd), *korola* (bitter gourd), *kakrul* (spicy gourd) and *potol* (pointed gourd). These do appear at Asian greengrocers from time to time and you should buy them if you can.

The dishes in this chapter are prepared by a number of different cooking processes which include the *bhoortha*, *niramish*, *tarkari*, *dalna*, *dolma* – and the *bhaji* (or *vhaji*) methods. Pronounced 'vargee' in Bangladeshi, the last is a light stir-fry of any chopped or shredded vegetables in a little oil with a pinch of turmeric. At the curry houses, this term has in one particular instance been confused with another process – the *bhajia*. Also called *pakora*, this is a batter based deep-fried fritter. The onion *bhajia* (usually misnamed *barjee*) is the best example (see page 50).

Bangladeshis can on the whole get along without *dal* or lentils. This cannot be said for their neighbours in India's West Bengal. In fact, one major lentil, the yellow *cholar* or *chana* even goes under the name 'gram' or Bengal 'gram'. It is indigenous to the area and, of course, becomes the gram flour indispensable to *pakoras* and the onion bhajia.

The three pulse recipes, apart from being distinctively delicious, also allow me to demonstrate three more Bangladeshi processes – the *charchuri* (dry-fry), *tok* (sour tastes) and *shukto* (bitter tastes).

Bangladeshis are not by definition vegetarian. Meat and poultry are eaten as and when possible, and fish and shellfish are ubiquitous. But although a Bangladeshi meal could be considered complete without meat or poultry, it would not be served without two or three vegetable dishes. One might be dry-fried, the other sweetish and a third spicy or sour.

With such a rich choice of vegetable dishes, of which this is only a representative selection, it is easy to see why they are so popular.

Lal Shak

RED SPINACH

•

LAL SHAK is a particular kind of Bangladeshi leaf. It is also common in India where it is called *lal sag* or *lal chauli* in Hindi and Urdu and *mulai keerai* in the south (Tamil). *Lal* means 'red', and the leaves, from the amaranth plant (*Amaranthus gangeticus*), are equally adored by the Chinese. Known also as Chinese spinach (*Yin Tsoi*), the leaves are dark crimson red, tinged with dark green, and are often available from Asian greengrocers. Failing that, use spinach beet or rhubarb chard leaves or red mountain spinach which are different in flavour, but not in colour. The cooking is really light, the result a delight. Do not confuse rhubarb chard with rhubarb whose leaves are poisonous.

——— SERVES 4 as an accompaniment ———

1 lb (450 g) fresh lal shak leaves and tender stalks	½ teaspoon dry red chilli seeds
	1 oz (25 g) Garlic Tarka (see page 31)
2 tablespoons mustard blend oil	4 oz (110 g) Onion Tarka (see page 32)
½ teaspoon Panch Foran (see page 36)	salt to taste

1. Wash and chop the leaves and stalks, then boil, steam or microwave them to tender but do not over-cook.

2. Heat the oil in a karahi or wok. Stir-fry the panch foran and chilli seeds for 20 seconds. Add the garlic and onion tarka (or slow cook them from scratch for 15–20 minutes).

3. Add the cooked hot leaves and stalks. Stir well, add salt to taste and serve.

Puishak or Puishag

JUTE LEAVES

•

THE young leaves of the jute plant – *puishak* (see page 95) – are tender and a little spinach-like in taste and in colour when cooked. Called *patsag* or *patuasag* in Hindi/Urdu they are available, in season, at Asian greengrocers.

My effective substitute is young spinach and rocket. High in iron, this dish is another lightly cooked ace from Bangladesh.

——— SERVES 4 as an accompaniment ———

1 lb (450 g) fresh puishak leaves and tender stalks or 10 oz (300 g) baby young spinach and 6 oz (175 g) rocket
2 tablespoons mustard blend oil
$\frac{1}{2}$ teaspoon white cummin seeds
$\frac{1}{3}$ teaspoon white poppy seeds
$\frac{1}{4}$ teaspoon lovage seeds (ajwain)
$\frac{1}{2}$ teaspoon dry red chilli seeds
1 oz (25 g) Garlic Tarka (see page 32)
4 oz (110 g) Onion Tarka (see page 31)
salt to taste

1. Wash and chop the leaves and stalks, then boil, steam or microwave them to tender but do not over-cook.

2. Heat the oil in a karahi or wok. Stir-fry the seeds for 20 seconds. Add the garlic and onion tarka (or slow cook them from scratch for 15–20 minutes).

3. Add the cooked hot leaves. Stir well, add salt to taste and serve.

Korola Bhoortha

SPICY 'BITTER' GOURD SALAD

•

THE bitter gourd or cucumber *korola*, or *karela* as it is called in Hindi/Urdu, was named after Kerala, India's most southerly state, by the seventeenth-century Dutch governor Draaksteen in his book *Hortus Indicus Malabaricus*. Korola is bright green and knobbly, is on average about 6 inches (15 cm) by $1\frac{1}{2}$ inches (3.75 cm) and has sharp, pointed ends. It is readily available from Asian or Chinese greengrocers.

Bitter tastes are enjoyed by Bangladeshis and Indians, although much of the bitterness is 'leeched' out of the gourd by chopping it into tiny strips, then soaking it in salty water for an hour or two.

Added to other ingredients, the gourd's flavour, though acquired, is very delicate and leads one to want more. The dish can be served cold and raw, when it is soft and subtle with a 'young' taste or, as in the next two recipes it can be served hot. Then, the colour is darker and the tastes a little more mature and contrastingly different. Rasheed and Roosha served both together for lunch at their Sylhetti home. It was great.

——— **SERVES 4 as an accompaniment** ———

2 fresh korola (bitter gourds)	2 oz (50 g) onion, cut into small strips
4 tablespoons salt	$\frac{1}{2}$ teaspoon Panch Foran (see page 36)
1–2 dry red chillies, chopped	1 garlic clove, very finely chopped
1–2 fresh green cayenne chillies, cut into rings	salt to taste

1. Cut the ends off the korolas and discard. Halve the korolas and discard the seeds in the centre. Then cut the gourds into approx. $1 \times \frac{1}{4}$ inch (2.5 × 6 mm) strips.

2. Put the strips into a non-metallic bowl. Sprinkle the salt in, then add enough cold water to cover the strips.

3. Cover the bowl and leave to stand for an hour or two.

4. Drain and rinse the strips. Then, in the same bowl, add all the remaining ingredients except the salt to taste. Mix well and cover again.

5. Leave in the fridge for a couple more hours, then add salt to taste and serve chilled.

Korola Bhoortha Jal

FRIED SPICY BITTER GOURD

•

SIMPLY stir-fry the mixture in oil.

──────── SERVES 4 as an accompaniment ────────

1 quantity of Korola Bhoortha (see page 112)
3 tablespoons sunflower oil

½ teaspoon turmeric
salt to taste

1. Follow the instructions for Korola Bhoortha to Step 4.

2. Heat the oil in a karahi or wok. Stir-fry the turmeric for 30 seconds, then add the mixture for about 4 minutes.

3. Add salt to taste and serve.

Korola Bhaji (Vhaji) or Shukto
MIXED VEGETABLES WITH BITTER GOURD

•

ONCE more the 'bitter' gourd takes centre stage, this time with a supporting cast of potatoes, garlic, ginger and spices. This is also called *shuktoni* or *shukti*, meaning sour or bitter curry, and other vegetables including aubergine, potol, plantain and spinach can be added. Bitterness is not only enjoyed in Bangladesh, it is also considered good for the blood, and an anti-malariant.

——— SERVES 4 as an accompaniment ———

2 fresh tender korola (bitter gourds)
4 tablespoons salt
12 baby new potatoes
3 tablespoons vegetable ghee
2–3 garlic cloves, chopped
3 oz (75 g) plain yoghurt
10–12 fresh curry leaves (optional)
1 tablespoon chopped fresh coriander leaves
salt to taste

SPICES
1 teaspoon white cummin seeds
1 teaspoon white poppy seeds
$\frac{1}{2}$ teaspoon black onion seeds
$\frac{1}{2}$ teaspoon turmeric
2–3 bay leaves

1. Cut the ends off the korolas and discard. Halve the korolas and discard the seeds in the centre. Then cut the gourds into approx. $1 \times \frac{1}{4}$ inch (2.5 cm×6 mm) strips.

2. Put the strips into a non-metallic bowl. Sprinkle the salt in, then add enough cold water to cover the strips.

3. Cover the bowl and leave to stand for an hour or two.

4. Boil the new potatoes in their jackets (babies take about 10 minutes).

5. Meanwhile, heat the ghee in a karahi or wok. Stir-fry the **spices** for 30 seconds. Add the garlic and stir-fry for a further minute.

6. Drain and rinse the strips and add them to the mixture. Stir-fry for 2–3 minutes more.

7. Add the potatoes with the yoghurt, curry leaves and chopped coriander leaves. Stir well for a couple more minutes. Add salt to taste and serve.

OPPOSITE *Dohi Maach* (pomfret in yogurt, page 105). Note the pomfret in the background

Kakrul Jal (or *Potol Jal*)
FRIED SEEDED GOURD
•

KAKRUL is a small gourd about the shape and size of a lemon and bright lime-green in colour. Known as the spiny bitter cucumber or *kantola* or kakrul in Bangladesh, it has a long stalk and is covered in what look like tiny delicate spines or prickles – which turn out to be soft and unprickly.

Kakrul's flavour is somewhat nondescript and not as bitter as *korola*, but it should still be leeched in brine. Its texture is that of orange peel yet, when cooked, it is transformed. Eat it, seeds and all, with plain yoghurt or with other curries.

Kakruls do appear at Asian greengrocers from time to time. *Chichinga* – snake gourd – can be used instead, but its peel must be discarded. The recipe also works well using *potol* (pointed gourd see page 123) or courgette slices or baby white aubergines.

─────── SERVES 4 as an accompaniment ───────

4 kakruls (or potols, see above)
4 tablespoons mustard blend oil
1 teaspoon sugar
salt
crispy Onion Tarka (see page 31) to garnish

SPICES
$\frac{1}{4}$ teaspoon turmeric
$\frac{1}{4}$ teaspoon yellow mustard powder
$\frac{1}{4}$ teaspoon chilli powder

1. Wash the kakruls, then put them whole into a non-metallic bowl. Sprinkle with 2 teaspoons salt, then cover with water and leave for 2–4 hours.

2. Drain, rinse and dry the kakruls, then slice them longways. They should be about $\frac{1}{2}$ inch (12 mm) or less thick.

3. Heat the oil in a large, flat frying pan and stir-fry the **spices** and sugar for 10 seconds.

4. Place the kakrul slices in the pan and, keeping them on the move, fry for about 5 minutes, turning to achieve even goldness. Sprinkle with salt to taste and garnish with the onion tarka.

OPPOSITE Top to bottom: *Korola Bhoortha* (cold spicy bitter gourd, page 112) and *Potol Jal* (fried seeded gourd, above). The vegetables (top right) are potol, fresh turmeric and korola. On the left is amla, a type of sour olive (see *Amla Achar*, page 152)

Kakrul Bhaji (Vhaji)
SEEDED GOURD CURRY

•

KAKRUL makes an interesting light curry or *bhaji* (pronounced 'varjee'). Serve hot with other curries and rice. Again, courgettes or baby white aubergines can be substituted.

——— SERVES 4 as an accompaniment ———

4–6 kakruls
salt
4 tablespoons sunflower oil
$\frac{1}{2}$ teaspoon turmeric
1 teaspoon chilli powder

4 garlic cloves, finely chopped
1 teaspoon Panch Foran (see page 36)
4 oz (110 g) onion, very finely chopped
1 tablespoon chopped fresh coriander
  leaves

1. Wash the kakruls, then put them whole into a non-metallic bowl. Sprinkle with 2 teaspoons salt, then cover with water and leave for 2–4 hours (to leech out the bitterness).

2. Drain, rinse and dry the kakruls, then slice them into strips, skin and seeds included, about $1 \times \frac{1}{3}$ inch (2.5 cm × 8 mm) thick.

3. Heat the oil in a karahi or wok and stir-fry the turmeric and chilli powder for 30 seconds. Add the garlic and panch foran and stir-fry for a further 20 seconds.

4. Add the onion and stir-fry for about 5 minutes.

5. Add about 4 fl oz (100 ml) water and, when simmering, add the kakrul.

6. Simmer for 3–4 minutes. Add the chopped coriander leaves and salt to taste.

7. Simmer for a couple more minutes, then serve.

Tarkari Vhaji

MIXED VEGETABLE CURRY

•

IN THIS case I am using potatoes and long beans – those pale green beans that are 1–3 feet (30–90 cm) long and sold in coils at Asian stores. Kenyan/French beans can be substituted.

Note the absence of garlic in this *tarkari*, which gets its name from the onion tarka that is added to the curry at the end of cooking.

——— SERVES 4 as an accompaniment ———

4 large potatoes
1 teaspoon turmeric
8 oz (225 g) long beans
2 inch (5 cm) piece fresh ginger
2–3 fresh green cayenne chillies
3 tablespoons sunflower oil
10–12 fresh or dried curry leaves
1 tablespoon brown sugar
2 teaspoons Bangladeshi Garam Masala (see page 34)

8 oz (225 g) cooked Onion Tarka (see page 31)
salt to taste

SPICES
$\frac{1}{2}$ teaspoon turmeric
1 teaspoon chilli powder
$\frac{1}{2}$ teaspoon black mustard seeds

1. Peel and quarter the potatoes and three-quarters cook them in boiling water with the turmeric. They should be soft when poked with a thin sharp knife yet still resistant. Strain them, retaining 8 fl oz (225 ml) of the water.

2. Wash and string (if necessary) the long beans and cut them into 4 inch (10 cm) lengths.

3. Mulch the **spices**, ginger and chillies in a food processor, using just enough water to achieve a pourable paste.

4. Heat the oil in a karahi or wok. Stir-fry the paste for about a minute. Add the beans and continue to stir-fry for a couple of minutes to coat them with the spices.

5. Add the potato water and the potatoes. Stir and simmer for 5 minutes.

6. Add the curry leaves, sugar and garam masala, and stir and simmer for a couple more minutes.

7. Add the onion tarka, stir in well, add salt to taste and serve.

Narish's Begoomi Pakora

AUBERGINE FRITTERS

•

SMALL, purply-black aubergines make ideal *pakoras* when sliced, battered and deep-fried. They can be used as starters, but are even better, in my experience, as a crispy vegetable side dish accompanying other curries and rice. My experience in this case was a delightful dinner party in Sylhet given by Narish and her family. This is one of her recipes.

——— SERVES 4 as an accompaniment ———

4–6 small black aubergines, each about
   4 inches (10 cm) long
oil for deep-frying

BATTER
4 oz (110 g) gram flour (besan) or 2 oz (50 g)
   gram flour and 2 oz (50 g) plain flour
1 egg
3 oz (75 g) plain yoghurt
1 tablespoon fresh or bottled lemon juice
1 teaspoon salt

$\frac{1}{2}$ teaspoon lovage seeds (ajwain)
2 teaspoons Bangladeshi Garam Masala (see
   page 34)
2 teaspoons dried fenugreek leaves
$\frac{1}{2}$–2 teaspoons chilli powder

GARNISH
Bangladeshi Garam Masala (see page 34)
rock salt
Cox's Bazaar Hot Sprinkler (see page 37)
fresh coriander leaves

1. Mix the batter ingredients to achieve a thickish paste which will drop sluggishly off the spoon. Let it stand for at least 10 minutes, during which time the mixture will absorb the moisture.

2. Cut the stalky tops off the aubergines, then slice the aubergines longways, into discs about $\frac{1}{4}$ inch (6 mm) thick.

3. Put all the discs into the batter and ensure they are all coated.

4. Pre-heat the oil in the deep-fryer to 375°F/190°C (chip-frying temperature).

5. One by one, carefully place the discs in the hot oil. Doing it slowly will maintain the oil temperature.

6. Deep-fry for 8–10 minutes, turning once. Remove from the oil, sprinkle on the garam masala, rock salt, hot sprinkler and fresh coriander leaves and serve at once.

Khatta or Ambal Begoom

SLICED AUBERGINE IN A SWEET SAUCE

•

KHATTA literally means 'sour' in Bangladeshi and, as I have mentioned before, is a taste particularly enjoyed there. Actually this much loved dish, also called *ambal*, is as much sweet as sour.

─── SERVES 4 ───

4–6 small, black-skinned aubergines, each about 4–5 inches (10–12.5 cm) long
4 tablespoons sunflower oil
2 tablespoons vegetable ghee
1 teaspoon Panch Foran (see page 36)
1 teaspoon chopped dried red chilli
1 fresh red chilli, cut into rings
4 tablespoons sugar
1 teaspoon Tamarind Purée (see page 38)
1 teaspoon bottled sweet mango chutney syrup

2 teaspoons tomato ketchup
salt to taste

GARNISH
3–4 tablespoons crispy Onion Tarka (see page 31)
fresh coriander leaves

SPICES
$\frac{1}{2}$ teaspoon chilli powder
$\frac{1}{2}$ teaspoon ground coriander
$\frac{1}{3}$ teaspoon ground cinnamon

1. Cut the stalks off the aubergines and slice the aubergines diagonally longways (or into rounds) to about $\frac{1}{4}$ inch (6 mm) thick. Soak them in salty water for about 30 minutes. Drain and dry.

2. Using just sufficient water, make a fairly runny paste of the **spices**.

3. Coat the aubergine slices with the paste.

4. Heat the oil in a large, flat frying pan. Fry the aubergine slices on a lowish heat for about 5–6 minutes a side.

5. Meanwhile, heat the ghee in a karahi or wok. Stir-fry the panch foran and dried and fresh chillies for 30 seconds. Add 3 fl oz (75 ml) water and, when simmering, add the sugar. Stir-fry until it starts to thicken into a syrup.

6. Add the tamarind, mango chutney syrup and tomato ketchup and, when sizzling, the aubergine slices. Stir-fry for just enough time to ensure the slices are hot. Add salt to taste.

7. Arrange the slices on a serving dish. Pour all the remaining syrup over them and garnish with the onion tarka, and fresh coriander leaves.

Niramish

BANGLADESHI MIXED VEGETABLE CURRY

•

A VEGAN, or true vegetarian dish (it contains no butter or dairy products), *niramish* is found exclusively in Bangladesh. It is also unusual in that garlic, ginger and onions are not used.

Panch Foran is fried in mustard blend oil, a little sugar is optional and lentils can be incorporated, as they are in this attractive version, in which I have used only quick-to-cook 'European' vegetables. In fact, apart from leaf vegetables, any single vegetable or combination of vegetables, 'European' or 'exotic' is acceptable. Try this for flavour first. Another tasty combination includes parsnip, sweet potatoes and peas, although it takes longer to cook these vegetables.

Next time try it with your own choice of vegetable(s).

———— SERVES 4 ————

4 tablespoons mustard blend oil
1 teaspoon Panch Foran (see page 36)
2–3 bay leaves
4 oz (110 g) frozen peas, thawed
4 oz (110 g) carrot, chopped into cubes
4 oz (110 g) celery, chopped
4 oz (110 g) sweetcorn
4 oz (110 g) courgette, cut into slices
1–2 fresh red chillies, chopped

2 tablespoons cooked lentils (optional)
2 teaspoons sugar (optional)
salt to taste

SPICES
$\frac{1}{2}$ teaspoon turmeric
1 teaspoon chilli powder
1 teaspoon ground coriander

1. Heat the oil in a karahi or wok. Stir-fry the **spices**, panch foran and bay leaves for 30 seconds.

2. Add the vegetables and chillies and stir-fry for about 2 minutes.

3. Add about 6 fl oz (175 ml) water and stir to the simmer, cooking for about 6 minutes.

4. Add the lentils and sugar if using. Add salt to taste and serve at once.

Rangalu Kanchkala Dom

SWEET POTATO AND GREEN BANANA CURRY
•

THE *dom* process is cooking by steaming. Bananas as a very popular Bangladeshi vegetable and every part – the flesh (*kala*), the stem (*thora*) and the flower (*mochar*), when it is in season – is eaten. Even the leaves are used.

The bananas themselves grow in clusters on a long stem which hangs down from their tree. At the bottom of the stem, at a certain time of year, the plant flowers. The 'flower' grows to about 8 inches (20 cm) in length and is like an elongated heart shape, surrounded by purple-brown leaves. Under the leaves are florets, and yellow stigma. The florets are edible and highly prized. Banana flowers are occasionally available in the West.

Cooking plantains or green bananas (*kanchkala*) certainly are available, so use them in this recipe – but should their flowers come to hand, add them instead of the sweet potato (*rangalu*).

—— SERVES 4 ——

3–4 large, ripe, yellow-green
  plantains
8 oz (225 g) red sweet potatoes
3 tablespoons sunflower oil
2 teaspoons white cummin seeds
4 oz (110 g) onion, chopped
2 fresh red chillies, chopped
2–3 bay leaves

1 teaspoon sugar
salt to taste

SPICES
1 teaspoon ground coriander
1 teaspoon ground cinnamon
$\frac{1}{2}$ teaspoon turmeric
$\frac{1}{2}$ teaspoon chilli powder

1. Peel the plantains and cut them into large bite-sized pieces. Peel and cube the sweet potatoes.

2. Using a bamboo steamer, or a close-fitting sieve above a pan of boiling water, steam the plantain and potato cubes for 10–15 minutes. Test for tenderness.

3. Meanwhile, heat the oil in a karahi or wok. Stir-fry the cummin seeds and **spices** for 30 seconds, then add the onion, chillies and bay leaves and, on a low heat, slowly cook to a tarka (see note) over 15 minutes.

4. Add the steamed items and mix in well until sizzling. Add the sugar and salt to taste.

NOTE

Step 3 can be reduced in time to less than a minute, if you use the pre-made tarka described on page 31.

Derosh Charchuri

OKRA STIR-FRY

•

DEROSH is Bangladeshi for okra. It is also known as ladies' fingers or *bindi* in Hindi/Urdu or *vendaikai* in Tamil. At the curry house it is best known as *bindi bhajee.*

Okra are rather difficult to cook. The first factor is careful selection. It is usually better to choose smaller ones – the large ones are often scaly. Do not cook them in water as they will ooze sap while cooking. Even slight over-cooking results in a soggy mush and again that sticky sap. It is most unpleasant, and unfortunately this is one of those dishes which many standard curry restaurants get wrong. It can only be successful if it is cooked fresh. Here it is stir-fried in the *charchuri* or dry-fry method.

——— SERVES 4 ———

1 lb (450 g) okra
6 tablespoons mustard blend oil
2 teaspoons black mustard seeds
½ teaspoon black cummin seeds
4 tablespoons chopped onion (preferably use a small pink one for flavour and colour)
2 tomatoes, finely chopped
1 tablespoon chopped red bell pepper
2–3 fresh green chillies, chopped
1 tablespoon brown sugar
juice of 1 lemon

1 tablespoon chopped fresh coriander leaves
salt to taste

SPICES
½ teaspoon turmeric
1 teaspoon ground cummin
1 teaspoon ground coriander
½ teaspoon chilli powder
1 teaspoon ground cassia bark
½ teaspoon green cardamom seeds (not pods)

1. Carefully (so as not to damage them) wash the okra. Do not trim yet.

2. Heat the oil in a karahi or wok. Stir-fry the seeds for 30 seconds, then add the onion and stir-fry for 5 minutes.

3. Add the tomatoes, pepper, chillies and sugar and stir-fry for 5 minutes.

4. Meanwhile, chop the okra into 1 inch (2.5 cm) pieces, add them to the karahi straightaway, and gently toss for 5 minutes.

5. Add the lemon juice and **spices** with the chopped coriander leaves.

6. Stir-fry carefully for 5 minutes more. If the okra were tender to start with they are now cooked perfectly. Add salt to taste and serve at once. Do not store or freeze this dish – it will go sappy and mushy.

Chichinga Potol Jal
STIR-FRIED GOURD CURRY
·

THIS absolutely authentic, much adored Bangladeshi stir-fry uses *chichinga*, a long, thin, curly gourd aptly called the 'snake gourd' and *potol* (or *patol*, known as *parwal* in Hindi), for which I can find only one English translation – 'pointed gourd'. The best way to describe potol's shape is to call it a miniature rugby ball ranging in length between 3 and 6 inches (7.5 and 15 cm). A miniature version up to 2 inches (5 cm) long is called *tinda* or *tindora* and can also be used. Both vegetables are bright green with pale, longitudinal stripes and are regularly available at Asian greengrocers.

Chichinga can grow to several feet long, hangs down from its plant, and is totally snake-like in appearance – complete with pointed tail. Normally it is between 8 and 10 inches (20 and 25 cm) long, and it can be curled up.

On our recent trip to Bangladesh a general strike on our last day there immobilised Dhaka. Originated by Gandhi as a non-violent demonstration, the strike is called a *hartal*. For our own prudence we confined ourselves in the Skyline Hotel near the airport for 36 hours, to await our flight out. But we greatly enjoyed the room service meals of Bangladeshi curries. This was one of the dishes. We observed that we were holed up through the *hartal* in our hotel eating *potol*.

——— SERVES 4 ———

3–4 potol gourds	$\frac{1}{2}$ teaspoon turmeric
1 × 10 inch (25 cm) chichinga gourd	1–2 red chillies, cut into rings
4 tablespoons sunflower oil	2 fl oz (50 ml) milk
1 teaspoon black mustard seeds	8 oz (225 g) Onion Tarka (see page 31)
1 teaspoon Panch Foran (see page 36)	salt to taste

1. Peel the gourds and halve and de-seed them. Chop them into small pieces. Blanch them to nearly tender.

2. Heat the oil in a karahi or wok. Stir-fry the mustard seeds, panch foran and turmeric for 30 seconds. Add the chillies and the gourds and stir-fry for a couple of minutes.

3. Add the milk and stir well until it simmers.

4. Stir-fry for about 5 minutes. Check that the gourds are tender (some may take a little longer). Add the onion tarka and salt to taste. Serve hot.

Alu Kopir Motor Dalna
POTATO, CAULIFLOWER AND PEA CURRY
•

THE *dalna* process is unique to West and East Bengal, the latter now Bangladesh of course. The subject is nearly always mixed vegetables (the above being a traditional and favourite combination). They are fried with garlic/ginger paste and onion (cooked to a *tarka*). So far this is standard. The clue to the distinctive feature of the dalna is the fact that it is a Bengali speciality. Remember their sweet tooth? Towards the end a little water, white molasses or sugar is added and stir-fried on a high heat.

A little yoghurt or coconut milk is often added to make things creamy.

———— SERVES 4 ————

6 tablespoons sunflower oil
3–4 garlic cloves, very finely chopped
1 inch (2.5 cm) piece fresh ginger, very finely chopped
8 oz (225 g) onions, very finely chopped
2–3 fresh green chillies, sliced
1 tablespoon white molasses or white sugar
8 oz (225 g) boiled, peeled potatoes, diced into bite-sized pieces
8 oz (225 g) cauliflower florets, blanched until nearly tender

8 oz (225 g) frozen peas, thawed
6 tablespoons home-made yoghurt or
  6 tablespoons coconut milk
salt to taste

SPICES
1 teaspoon turmeric
1 teaspoon chilli powder
1 teaspoon Bangladeshi Garam Masala (see page 34)
2 bay leaves
2 teaspoons ground coriander

1. Heat the oil in a karahi or wok.

2. Add the **spices** and stir-fry for 30 seconds. Add the garlic and ginger, lower the heat, and obtain a golden brown tarka over about 5 minutes.

3. Add the onion and chillies and continue stir-frying on a low heat (just sizzling) to continue the tarka, taking around 15 minutes.

4. Raise the heat and when the tarka is hot, add the molasses or sugar and just enough water to enable it to melt and become a syrup.

5. Add the vegetables, mixing in well. As soon as the vegetables start to sizzle add the yoghurt or coconut milk and salt to taste. Serve at once.

NOTE
Steps 2 and 3 can be reduced in time to less than a minute, if you use the pre-made tarkas described on pages 31 and 32.

Begoomi Dolma
STUFFED AUBERGINES (EGGPLANTS)
•

ALL THE countries of the Middle East have their *dolma* items, which can be traced back to before 1000 BC. Just how the dolma entered Bengal whilst avoiding India is an interesting speculation. Presumably it came with early Moslem invaders. But it is there, and it is popular.

Dolma literally means 'to stuff' (vegetables), and any suitable vegetable can be stuffed – artichokes, marrows, courgettes, cabbage leaves, vine leaves, potatoes, tomatoes and peppers.

Here are two dolmas: aubergine in this recipe and bitter gourd in the next. Use any of the three spicy stuffings from pages 40, 42 and 46 – vegetable, mince (*keema*) or *alu motor* (potato and peas) – or use leftover cooked rice from Chapter 7. Bangladeshi stuffing is, of course, much spicier than that of the Middle East! Exactly how much you use depends on the exact size of the vegetable itself, and of its cavity.

Serve with a gravy such as the kofta gravy on page 107 if you wish.

——— **MAKES 4 dolmas** ———

4 × 8 inch (20 cm) black-skinned aubergines
vegetable (shobji) filling (see page 40) or
  mince (keema) filling (see page 42) or

potato and peas (alu motor) filling (see page 46)
2–3 tablespoons melted ghee

1. Pre-heat the oven to 375°F/190°C/Gas Mark 5.

2. Wash the aubergines, cut off the tops and bottoms, but leave the skin on.

3. Using a small long sharp knife carefully cut down from the stalk end to remove the core. Discard the pith and seeds.

4. Stuff the cavity.

5. Line an oven tray with foil and brush with ghee.

6. Put the stuffed aubergines upright (core vertical) on to the foil and into the oven.

7. Bake for 15–20 minutes, basting at least once with ghee from the tray.

8. Serve hot.

Korola Dolma

STUFFED BITTER GOURDS

•

A VARIATION on the previous recipe. You can, of course, use any of the vegetables mentioned in the previous introductions or even some that have not been mentioned. For example, use green bananas, skin on, or *shaktora* (see page 54), even oranges or lemons!

———— MAKES 4 dolmas ————

4 × 6 inch (15 cm) korolas
vegetable (shobji) filling (see page 40) or
   mince (keema) filling (see page 42) or

potato and peas (alu motor) filling (see
   page 46)
2–3 tablespoons melted ghee

1. Slit the gourds longways and carefully remove the central pith and seeds. Soak the gourds in a large bowl of salty water for 1–2 hours (see page 112).

2. Pre-heat the oven to 375°F/190°C/Gas Mark 5.

3. Drain and rinse the gourds, and carefully dry them inside and outside. Put the stuffing into the cavities.

4. Line an oven tray with foil and brush with ghee. Put the stuffed gourds on to the foil and into the oven. Bake for 15–20 minutes, basting at least once with ghee from the tray. Serve hot.

Shukta Cholar

GOURDS WITH BENGAL GRAM (CHANA DAL)

•

GOURD mixed with lentils is a popular combination dish in Bengal and Bangladesh. Any kind of gourd and any kind of lentil works well. Here I've used *chola* or *chana*. Green *moong* or black *urid* can substitute. A typical local touch is the addition of sultanas to give the dish a sweet punctuation. Personally I can live without this, so I've called it optional. I can't live without the sharp taste this dish should have, so leave in the lemon juice and lime pickle. Better still, use some of your own *amla* pickle instead (see page 152).

——— SERVES 4 ———

5 oz (150 g) yellow gram cholar (chana) lentils, split and polished
1 lb (450 g) marrow, courgettes or any type of gourd
6 tablespoons mustard blend oil
3–4 garlic cloves, sliced
4–6 spring onions, leaves and bulbs, chopped
2–3 fresh red chillies, sliced
1–2 tablespoons sultanas (optional)
1 tablespoon amla pickle flesh or lime pickle, finely chopped
10–12 fresh or dried curry leaves

2 tablespoons ghee
salt to taste
1 tablespoon chopped fresh coriander leaves

SPICES
$\frac{1}{2}$ teaspoon turmeric
1 teaspoon celery seeds (radhuni)
1 teaspoon black mustard seeds
$\frac{1}{2}$ teaspoon ground coriander
$\frac{1}{2}$ teaspoon Bangladeshi Garam Masala (see page 34)
$\frac{1}{2}$ teaspoon ground cinnamon

1. Pick through the lentils to remove any grit or impurities. Rinse them several times, then drain and immerse in ample water for 4–12 hours.

2. Drain and rinse the lentils, then measure an amount of water, twice their volume, into a 4 pint (2.25 litre) saucepan. Bring to the boil.

3. Add the lentils and simmer for about 30 minutes, stirring from time to time and adding a little more water if needed. The water should be absorbed totally into the lentils, which should be quite soft, almost puréed.

4. Wash the gourds. Discard the peel if it is coarse (but retain if using courgettes or korola, etc). Discard pith and seeds. Chop the vegetables into delicate bite-sized pieces.

5. Timing this stage carefully, steam or microwave the pieces to tender so that they can be added hot to the stir-fry at the end of Step 8.

6. Heat the oil in a karahi or wok. Stir-fry the **spices** for 15 seconds. Add the garlic and stir for about 1 minute more. Add the spring onions, lower the heat and stir-fry for a couple of minutes more.

7. Add the chillies, sultanas if using, pickle and curry leaves and a little water, stir-frying for 2–3 minutes. Keep 2 tablespoons of this mix aside for garnish.

8. Add the drained lentils and the ghee and stir-fry until the lentils are hot right through. Add the gourds.

9. Add salt to taste and the chopped coriander leaves.

10. Garnish with the 2 tablespoons of tarka saved earlier and serve.

Motor Dal Charchuri

DRY COOKED YELLOW SPLIT PEAS

•

YELLOW split peas (*motor dal*) are larger than split *chana* (*cholar dal*) and smaller than chick peas (*kabuli cholar*), though any one could be substituted in this recipe.

This *charchuri* (or *chach chori*) method of curry (which we met on page 122) is a kind of dry-fry, like the *bhoona* but less spicy. The spicing can vary to choice but usually includes at least some panch foran. Turmeric and chilli are mandatory. White poppy seeds (*posto*) are sometimes present, helping to 'dry out' the dish and to give a crunchier texture, and sugar is rarely omitted. Little if any water should be used. Any ingredient can be cooked by this method.

The yellow split peas in this recipe are pre-cooked to a chewy (not mushy) texture, then drained and left to dry out a little. The dish looks bright and golden, tastes as good as it looks and is a highlight on Dhaka's Sonagaon hotel's restaurant menu.

It is a meal in itself, served with rice or bread and chutneys and pickles, or it can be joined by other curries.

———— SERVES 4 ————

8 oz (225 g) polished yellow split peas
4–6 tablespoons sunflower oil
$\frac{1}{2}$ teaspoon turmeric
$\frac{1}{2}$ teaspoon chilli powder
1 teaspoon Panch Foran (see page 36)
2 teaspoons white poppy seeds
$\frac{1}{2}$–1 teaspoon chopped dry red chilli
2–3 garlic cloves, sliced
8 oz (225 g) onions, very finely chopped

2 tablespoons thin (julienne) strips red bell pepper
$\frac{1}{2}$–1 tablespoon chopped fresh red chilli
2–3 tablespoons vegetable ghee
1–2 teaspoons sugar
salt to taste
1 tablespoon chopped fresh coriander leaves

1. Pick through the peas to remove any grit or impurities. Rinse them several times, then drain and immerse in ample water for 12–24 hours.

2. Drain and rinse the peas then measure an amount of water, twice their volume, into a 4 pint (2.25 litre) saucepan. Bring to the boil.

3. Add the peas and simmer for about 40 minutes, stirring from time to time and adding a little more water if needed. Drain the peas when they are suitably chewy (not over-cooked) and set aside.

4. Heat the oil in a karahi or wok. Stir-fry the turmeric and chilli powder for 15 seconds. Add the panch foran, poppy seeds and dry chilli and stir-fry for 15 seconds. Add the garlic and stir-fry for about 1 minute more.

5. Add the onions, lower the heat and stir-fry for at least 5 minutes (more is better) to achieve a golden tarka (see page 31).

6. Add the red pepper and fresh chilli during this process. Keep 2 tablespoons of this mix aside for garnish.

7. Add the drained peas, the ghee and the sugar and stir-fry until the peas are hot right through.

8. Add salt to taste and the chopped coriander leaves.

9. Garnish with the 2 tablespoons of tarka saved earlier and serve.

—— *Variation* ——

Motor Shuti Charchori Use dried green split peas instead of yellow split peas. The green colour of the finished dish is unexpected and pleasing.

Razma Dal

RED KIDNEY BEAN CURRY

•

Although the subcontinent has a huge list of pulses that dates back to the earliest years, red kidney beans were not among them. Native to South America, they found their way to Europe in the sixteenth century. It was not until later that the French took them to India and grew them in Pondichery, in the south. The British took them northwards as late as the nineteenth century. It did not take the native population long to catch on. Being a pulse-loving nation, they found many ways to spice up the red kidney bean. Called *rajhma* in Hindi/Urdu and *razma* (or *barbati*) in Bengali, this recipe shows how delightful a simple staple can be. Serve with plain rice or bread and a tart pickle.

––––––– SERVES 4 –––––––

8 oz (225 g) red kidney beans
4 tablespoons ghee
4–6 garlic cloves, chopped
1–2 fresh red chillies, sliced
1–2 fresh green chillies, cut into rings
1 tablespoon brown sugar
1 tablespoon tomato purée
1 tablespoon tomato ketchup
7 fl oz (200 ml) tinned coconut milk
1 tablespoon chopped fresh mint leaves
2 teaspoons Bangladeshi Garam Masala (see page 34)
salt to taste
crispy Onion Tarka (see page 31) to garnish

lemon wedges to serve

SPICES 1
2–3 bay leaves
12 cloves
6 green cardamom pods
2 brown cardamom pods
1 × 2 inch (5 cm) piece cassia bark

SPICES 2
$\frac{1}{2}$ teaspoon turmeric
1 teaspoon Panch Foran (see page 36)
2 teaspoons ground coriander
$\frac{1}{2}$ teaspoon ground cummin
2 teaspoons white sesame seeds

1. Pick through the beans to remove any grit or impurities. Rinse them several times, then drain and immerse in ample water for 12–24 hours.

2. Bring 2 pints (1.2 litres) water to the boil in a 4 pint (2.25 litre) saucepan. Drain and rinse the beans then add them to the saucepan and bring the water back to boiling. Keep it at this temperature for 10 minutes. This destroys any toxins which may be present in the beans. Skim off any scum.

3. Lower the temperature to achieve a simmer. Add **spices 1** and simmer for 45–60 minutes. Test the beans are tender. Drain.

4. Heat the ghee in a karahi or wok. Stir-fry **spices 2** for 30 seconds. Add the garlic and stir-fry for a further minute.

5. Add the chillies, sugar and tomato purée and ketchup and, when sizzling, add the beans.

6. Stir-fry briskly until they are sizzling.

7. Add the coconut milk, mint leaves and garam masala and, when simmering, salt to taste.

8. Garnish with the onion tarka and serve with lemon wedges.

Tok Dal

TART TASTING LENTILS

•

Tok (sour) tastes are, as I've said several times before, immensely popular in Bangladesh. Tamarind is the main souring agent here and its gorgeously distinctive flavour is enhanced by two tricks from upmarket gourmet and Dhaka restaurateur Abu S. Alam. These are finely chopped or puréed mango pickle and a little yoghurt. A squeeze of lime juice sets it off perfectly. This dish freezes well so if this recipe makes too much – freeze the spares. Any small lentil will do. Here I've used *masoor*. See also Tok Dal Soup on page 52.

─────── SERVES 4 ───────

8 oz (225 g) split and polished red *masoor* lentils
4 tablespoons sunflower or light oil
2–3 garlic cloves, chopped
6 oz (175 g) onions, sliced
1 tablespoon Tamarind Purée (see page 38)
1 tablespoon bottled mango pickle, very finely chopped or puréed

2 tablespoons plain yoghurt
salt to taste
lime wedges to serve

SPICES
½ teaspoon turmeric
½ teaspoon ground coriander
½ teaspoon ground cummin
½ teaspoon chilli powder

1. Pick through the lentils to remove any grit or impurities. Rinse them several times, then drain and immerse in ample water for 1–4 hours.

2. Drain and rinse the lentils, then measure an amount of water, twice their volume, into a 4 pint (2.25 litre) saucepan. Bring to the boil.

3. Add the lentils and simmer for about 40 minutes, stirring from time to time and adding a little more water if needed. The water should be absorbed totally into the lentils, which should be quite soft, almost puréed.

4. Heat the oil in a karahi or wok. Stir-fry the **spices** for 30 seconds. Add the garlic and onion and stir-fry for 5–10 minutes.

5. Add the stir-fry to the hot cooked lentils, with the tamarind, pickle and yoghurt. Mix well.

6. You can now add as much water as you wish to thin the mixture. When simmering, add salt to taste and serve with the lime wedges.

CHAPTER 7

✣ ◈ ✣

RICE

RICE IS Bangladesh's staple food. No Bangladeshi meal would be complete without it. According to Dr K.T. Achaya in his book *Indian Food*, published in Delhi by the Oxford University Press: 'A primitive wild aquatic grass is postulated to have existed in the huge land mass called Gondwanaland which, some 10 million years ago, split up to yield the present lands of Africa, India, Australia, and South America. The area including north-eastern India, northern Bangladesh, Burma, Thailand, Laos, Vietnam and southern China appears to be its place of origin. Thereafter the rice plant spread all over India wherever it encountered a fertile alluvial plain, encouraged in this by the efforts of humans attracted by its prolific grain yields.'

Bangladesh remains one of rice's natural growth areas. The land is easy to irrigate and paddy fields are everywhere. Even at flood time, although the silting of the fields can be overwhelmingly destructive, the rice not only thrives in most years but some varieties have adapted to deeper water by growing elongated stems.

Bangladesh has numerous varieties of rice, the best of which are *chinigura* or *kalijira*. These are fatter and very slightly more glutinous than Basmati rice (which is an import from India and available at a price). In fact, despite large harvests, Bangladesh is in the unenviable position of having annually to import 4 million tons of rice to make up its shortfall.

I recommend using Basmati rice in my recipes, although Thai fragranced rice is acceptably close to Bangladeshi varieties. Three processes of especial interest are the *kacchi* and the *tehari* methods on pages 136 and 138, and the cold rice dish with chillies on page 139.

All these recipes are enjoyed by Bangladeshis.

Siddha Chaul

PLAIN BOILED RICE

•

THIS can also be called *dheki chhata*, from the utensil it is cooked in.

This is the quickest way to cook rice, and it can be ready to serve in just 15 minutes from the water boiling. Two factors are crucial for this method to work perfectly. First, the rice must be Basmati rice. Patna or long-grained, quick-cook or other rices will require different timings and will have neither the texture nor the fragrance of Basmati. Second, it is one of the few recipes in this book which require *precision timing*. It is essential that for its few minutes on the boil you concentrate on it or else it may over-cook and become stodgy.

A 3 oz (75 g) portion of dry rice provides an ample helping per person; 2 oz (50 g) will be a smaller but adequate portion.

8–12 oz (225–350 g) Basmati rice
2–3 pints (1.2–1.75 litres) water

1. Pick through the rice to remove grit and impurities.

2. Boil the water. It is not necessary to salt it.

3. While it is heating up, rinse the rice briskly with fresh cold water until most of the starch is washed out. Run a kettle-full of hot water through the rice at the final rinse. This minimises the temperature reduction of the boiling water when you put the rice into it.

4. When the water is boiling properly, put the rice into the pan. Start timing. Put the lid on the pan until the water comes back to the boil, then remove the lid. It takes 8–10 minutes from the start. Stir frequently.

5. After about 6 minutes, taste a few grains. As soon as the centre is no longer brittle but still has a good *al dente* bite to it, put the rice in a strainer and drain off the water. The rice should seem slightly *under*-cooked.

6. Shake off all the excess water, then place the strainer on a dry tea towel which will help remove the last of the water.

7. After a minute place the rice in a warmed serving dish. You can serve it now or, preferably, put it into a very low oven or warming drawer for at least half an hour. As it dries, the grains will separate and become fluffy. It can be held in the warmer for several hours if needed.

Kabuli

CHICKEN AND PEA RICE

•

THIS dish is made using either Plain Boiled Rice (opposite) or Boiled Fragranced Rice (see page 138). Add peas and the chicken drumsticks, cooked as below, to the cooked rice. Tinned chick peas can be substituted for peas.

This is a meal in itself, so serve just with chutneys and pickles.

——— SERVES 4 ———

2 tablespoons butter ghee

4 cloves garlic, chopped

4 large or 8 small chicken drumsticks, skinned

6 fl oz (175 ml) akhni stock (see page 38) or water

2–3 bay leaves

2×2 inch (5 cm) pieces cassia bark

3 fl oz (75 ml) single cream

20–30 saffron strands

20 cashew nuts, chopped

1 tablespoon chopped fresh coriander leaves

2 teaspoons Bangladeshi Garam Masala (see page 34)

salt to taste

1 quantity cooked rice (see above)

3 oz (75 g) frozen peas, thawed

2 teaspoons rosewater

ample crispy Onion Tarka (see page 31)

SPICES

$\frac{1}{2}$ teaspoon white cummin seeds

$\frac{1}{2}$ teaspoon black cummin seeds

$\frac{1}{3}$ teaspoon turmeric

$\frac{1}{4}$ teaspoon ground cinnamon

$\frac{1}{2}$ teaspoon ground coriander

1. Heat the ghee in a karahi or wok. Stir-fry the **spices** with a little water for 1 minute. Add the garlic and stir-fry for a minute more.

2. Fry the drumsticks in this mixture for 2–3 minutes, turning and stirring.

3. Add the stock or water and the bay leaves and cassia bark and, when simmering, lower the heat and maintain the simmer for 10 minutes. Stir and turn the drumsticks from time to time.

4. Add the cream, saffron, cashew nuts, chopped coriander leaves and garam masala.

5. Simmer and stir for 5–10 minutes more (depending on drumstick size). Test that the flesh is cooked by poking with a sharp, slim knife and inspecting. Add salt to taste. Drain any spare liquid and keep for later.

6. Now carefully mix in the rice and the peas. Add salt to taste.

7. Bring to a gentle sizzle. Sprinkle with the rosewater, garnish with the onion tarka and serve with the spare liquid as gravy.

Kacchu Biriani

MEAT (OR VEGETABLE) COOKED RICE

•

THIS is a Moghul Moslem dish *par excellence*. The meat cooks with the rice from raw (*kacchu*), using enough stock to ensure that both not only cook to fragrant perfection, but also totally absorb the water and all the flavours.

The secret is really slow oven-cooking. In Bangladesh it is done in the waisted round metal pot called the *dheki*. It sits over the fire on the coals and the pot's lid is sealed with dough to prevent the escape of flavours.

I've seen it done at weddings in a *dheki* about 3 feet (1 metre) across – to feed 400 people. With a cooking time of 6 hours there was no room for error. Here we use a casserole dish, preferably the heavy cast-iron type, for just 3 hours in the oven. We will seal the lid with dough for authenticity.

There are a lot of variables at work here – actual oven temperature, density of rice, toughness of meat, hardness of water, etc. – but the dish won't end up either mushy or over-cooked. In the unlikely event that the meat needs a while longer, allow extra time (up to an hour) to return the pot back to the oven.

This is a meal in itself, of course, and a delicious one at that. Furthermore, it's not one which is practical in a restaurant. So unless you visit a Bangladeshi home and they serve it, you'll never know how good it is – until you cook it yourself!

──── SERVES 4 ────

1 lb (450 g) lean leg of lamb or fillet steak, weighed after Step 1
1 large potato
2×4 inch (10 cm) carrots
10 oz (300 g) Basmati rice
6 tablespoons butter ghee
4 garlic cloves, chopped
6 oz (175 g) onions, chopped
1 inch (2.5 cm) piece fresh ginger, chopped
2–3 fresh green chillies, sliced
1 pint (600 ml) akhni stock (see page 38) or water
20–30 saffron strands
4 fl oz (100 ml) single cream
1 tablespoon chopped fresh coriander leaves

1 teaspoon salt
dough (about half a batch from Unleavened Dough, page 142)

SPICES 1 (WHOLE SPICES)
6 green cardamom pods, crushed
2 brown cardamom pods, crushed
6 cloves
2×2 inch (5 cm) pieces cassia bark
1 teaspoon Panch Foran (see page 36)

SPICES 2 (GROUND SPICES)
$\frac{1}{2}$ teaspoon turmeric
$\frac{1}{2}$ teaspoon chilli powder
$1\frac{1}{2}$ teaspoons ground coriander
1 teaspoon ground cummin

1. Chop the meat into bite-sized cubes, and discard all unwanted matter.

2. Peel and quarter the potato and carrots.

3. Rinse the rice in several changes of cold water until it runs more or less clear. Then let it soak in ample water for about 20 minutes (to the end of Step 6).

4. Pre-heat the oven to 350°F/180°C/Gas Mark 4.

5. Use a lidded flameproof casserole dish large enough to allow for the expansion of the rice, that is, at least $9\frac{1}{2}$ pint (5.5 litre) capacity. Heat it on the stove. Add the ghee and, when this has melted, add **spices 1**. Stir-fry for 30 seconds then add **spices 2** and a little water. Stir-fry for 1 minute. Add the garlic, onions and ginger and stir-fry for about 5 minutes.

6. Drain the rice.

7. Add the meat and chillies and stir-fry for 5 minutes more.

8. Add the drained rice and stir-fry it into the mixture for a couple of minutes.

9. Add the stock or water and the vegetables, stir in, put the lid on and let it come to the boil (with luck about 3 minutes or so).

10. When it does, take the dish off the heat, add the saffron, cream and chopped coriander leaves and salt. Stir well.

11. Make the dough into a long sausage (or several short ones). Carefully (the pot's hot remember) fit the sausage all around the dish's rim. Gently push the lid down on to the sausage to form a seal. Don't press too hard or you'll push the dough aside.

12. Put the dish into the oven and leave it alone for at least 3 hours.

13. Then break the seal by removing the lid. Catch the waft of aromas (careful they're hot!) coming from the dish. Fork the biriani around to aerate it. (Discard the seal.)

14. Let the biriani rest, lid on, for up to 30 minutes to encourage separation, then fork again and serve with the garnish.

NOTE

For **Vegetable Kacchu Biriani**, omit the meat and use instead vegetables such as chopped sweet potato, green bananas and parsnips. The method remains the same.

Atap Chaul

BOILED FRAGRANCED RICE

·

THIS is a subtle variation on 'plain' boiled rice.

Use either Basmati rice of Thai fragranced rice. Follow the recipe on page 134 to the end, but put the cloves and bay leaves into the boiling water at Step 2. Sprinkle rosewater over the rice just before serving.

6 cloves
6 bay leaves
2 tablespoons rosewater

Gusht Tehari

MEAT FRIED RICE

·

THE *tehari* process is a Bangladeshi variety of *biriani* or *pullao* where meat is cooked with rice. Here, I am combining either Plain Boiled Rice (see page 134) or Boiled Fragranced Rice (see above) with the delicious Gomangse Bhoona from page 62. It's not quite the authentic way, but it is the way the curry restaurant makes it. And excellent it is, too. Traditionally tehari is a meal in itself, especially when served the traditional way with Bangladeshi Garnish (see page 150) and the unique Bangladeshi yoghurt drink – Borhani (see page 55).

——— **SERVES 4** ———

1 quantity cooked rice (see above)
1 quantity Gomangse Bhoona (see page 62)

1. Follow the recipe for plain boiled or fragranced rice in its entirety.

2. Follow the recipe for beef bhoona in its entirety. Note, however, that we only need to use between one-third and one-half of that recipe to get a good balance in the tehari, so freeze or fridge the spare.

3. Mix the two together, re-heating the mixture if necessary. Serve hot.

Morog Pullao

CHICKEN FRIED RICE

•

THIS is another 'assembly' job that combines one recipe with another to make a third. As I said in the previous recipe, it is the way curry restaurants do it. It is also done at home – sometimes just using up leftovers, other times from scratch. You can do it, too. Here it is from 'scratch'. It is easy to cut this recipe down to one-third or one-half quantities.

——— SERVES 4 ———

1 quantity Plain Boiled Rice (see page 134)
1 quantity Jhalfri Morog (see page 77)

1. Chop the chicken into bite-sized cubes, and discard all unwanted matter.

2. Follow the recipe for Jhalfri Morog in its entirety.

3. Mix the two together, re-heating the mixture if necessary. Serve hot.

Panta Bhat

WATER RICE

•

THIS is a cold dish, presumably devised to use up leftover plain rice. Serve it as a chutney-like accompaniment or even as an appetiser.

The rice quantity need only be an approximation; about a cupful is fine.

——— SERVES 4 as an accompaniment ———

About a cupful cold, cooked Plain Boiled Rice (see page 134)
1 teaspoon roasted black mustard seeds
$\frac{1}{3}$ teaspoon mango powder
2 spring onions, bulbs and leaves, chopped
1 fresh red chilli, cut into rings
salt to taste
crushed ice to serve

1. Put the rice into a bowl. Add all the other ingredients.

2. Cover with the same volume of water (about a cupful). Add some crushed ice and serve at once.

— *Variations* —

Add cold, cooked, chopped or mashed aubergine or some cold *korola* (see page 112).

Kitchuri

SPICY RICE WITH LENTILS

•

THIS is a delightful 'combination' dish with rice and lentils. It has been around in India, including Bengal, for centuries. In Calcutta and Dhaka, during the time of the British, it evolved into kedgeree in the hands of *Mog* Bengali cooks. Rice was combined with smoked haddock, boiled egg and pepper. It became a favourite breakfast food. Here is the Bangladeshi version of its forerunner – *kitchuri*. It is also called *khichadi*. Serve with a curry.

— SERVES 4 —

1 quantity Boiled Fragranced Rice (see page 138)
4 tablespoons ghee
2 garlic cloves, chopped
1–2 red chillies, chopped
2 oz (50 g) onion, very finely chopped
4 oz (110 g) cooked lentils from either of the recipes on pages 127–132

salt to taste

SPICES
1 teaspoon Panch Foran (see page 36)
$\frac{1}{2}$ teaspoon Bangladeshi Garam Masala (see page 34)
$\frac{1}{3}$ teaspoon turmeric

1. Follow the recipe for fragranced rice in its entirety.

2. Heat the ghee in a large karahi or wok. Stir-fry the **spices** for 30 seconds. Add the garlic, chillies and onion and stir-fry for about 5 minutes.

3. Add the cooked lentils and the rice. Stir-fry until all is blended and hot.

4. Add salt to taste.

CHAPTER 8

───── ⧉◈⧉ ─────

BREADS

WHEAT is not native to Bangladesh and so there is no bread-making tradition. Bread, as we know it, in the form of round, leavened loaves came to Bengal with the British and, to this day, that style of bread is popular with some Bangladeshis. You'll see fat loaves and French sticks in certain shops.

Real traditional 'bread' techniques have been imported from India, mostly in the form of flat unleavened discs of dough which are dry-cooked, pan-fried or deep-fried. Bear in mind that these are not normally offered with a Bangladeshi meal, and that when they are they will be made, more often than not, with that British inheritance, white flour. In Pakistan and northern India you will always encounter *ata* or *chupatti* flour. This brown flour, is finely milled from hard grains and is perfect for making Indian breads. Western stoneground/wholemeal flour is coarser and less glutinous, but can suffice.

Although Bangladeshi cooks in United Kingdom curry houses have mastered the making of *naan* bread in the *tandoor* oven (both of Afghan/Pakistani origin), this is not the case in Bangladesh itself. The tandoori is simply not there and nor, it seems, is the skill.

I have to let on that despite producing otherwise immaculate Bangladeshi food the naan breads served at Dhaka's topnotch and very expensive Sonar-gaon hotel were appalling.

For those who wish to make naan bread to accompany their Bangladeshi food, you will find definitive recipes for no less than 11 types in my book *Curry Club 100 Favourite Tandoori Recipes.*

Basic Dough-making

•

BEFORE we get down to the individual breads, it is important to study basic dough-making techniques. Once you have mastered the method you will confidently produce perfect bread. The principal secret to success lies in the first kneading or mixing of the basic ingredients: flour and water. This requires patient and steady mixing either by hand or by machine to transform the tacky mass of flour and water into a dough. It should be elastic without being sticky and should feel satisfying to handle. It should also be pliable, springy and soft.

This is the basic method for making unleavened dough.

UNLEAVENED DOUGH

Flour types and quantities are given in specific recipes.

1. Choose a large ceramic or glass bowl and put in the flour.

2. Add hot water little by little, and work it into the flour with your fingers. Soon it will become a lump.

3. Remove the lump from the bowl and knead it with your hand on a floured board or worktop until it is cohesive and well combined.

4. Return it to the bowl and leave it for 10–15 minutes, then briefly knead it once more. It will then be ready to use in the recipes.

Chupatti or Phulka

UNLEAVENED DRY BREAD, FLAT OR PUFFED

•

N OTHING could be simpler than the *chupatti*. It is just flour and water dough, rolled out to a thin 6–7 inch (15–18 cm) disc and cooked without oil on a hot, flat pan.

The *tava* (see page 16) is ideal but a flat frying pan will do. Note the trick to achieve the brown patches. This should also puff them out (the chupatti is then called the *phulka*). This recipe makes white flour chupattis, commonly encountered in Bangladesh. If you want brown ones, simply substitute brown *ata* or wholemeal flour for the strong white flour.

———— MAKES 4 chupattis ————

8 oz (225 g) strong white flour

1. Follow the recipe for unleavened dough opposite.

2. Divide the dough into four equal parts and shape each one into a ball. On a floured work surface, roll each ball into a thin disc about 6 inches (15 cm) in diameter.

3. Heat a tava or frying pan until very hot. Test it by dropping a tiny bit of flour on the bottom of the pan. If it turns brown at once the pan is ready.

4. Using no oil, cook the chupatti on one side for a minute or so. Turn it over and cook on the other side.

5. This may well produce brown patches. To accelerate this you can do what the natives do and (using tongs) dab the chupatti directly on to the hob. It works best with gas and next best with electric rings. It does not work with halogen or induction rings and makes a mess with a ceramic hob. Serve as hot and fresh as possible.

Loochi

WHITE FLOUR PURI

•

THE *puri* is a small, flat, unleavened white dough disc about 3–4 inches (7.5–10 cm) in diameter, which is deep-fried and, if you're lucky, puffs up into a crispy balloon. It is delicious as an alternative, or addition, to rice with curry. Or you can do what Bangladeshi kids do at tea-time and have the puris piping hot, just sprinkled with sugar and accompanied by a lovely cup of tea.

——— MAKES 16 puris ———

8 oz (225 g) strong white flour
1 tablespoon butter ghee

$\frac{1}{4}$ teaspoon salt
vegetable oil for deep-frying

1. Following the recipe for unleavened dough on page 142, mix the flour with water to make the dough. Add the ghee and salt at an early stage.

2. Divide the dough into four equal lumps and divide each lump into four to get 16 small, equal-sized lumps.

3. Shape each lump into a ball then, on a floured work surface, roll each ball into a small, thin disc about $3\frac{1}{2}$ inches (7.75 cm) in diameter.

4. Heat the oil in the deep-fryer to 375°F/190°C (chip-frying temperature) and immerse one disc in the oil. It will sink initially, then rise and, hopefully, puff up like a balloon. Turn it when it does this and remove after 30 seconds or so, when it should be golden. Shake off excess oil and keep the puri in a warming drawer or very low oven.

5. Repeat with the remaining puris. Serve as hot and fresh as possible.

—— *Variations* ——

Radha Bollobi (Gram Flour Puri) A Bengali variation of the Loochi. Simply substitute 8 oz (225 g) gram flour (besan) for plain flour. You can also add 1 teaspoon sugar if you wish. Follow the recipe above to make them.

Kochuri or Dhal Puri Add 2 oz (50 g) cooked lentils (*moong* or *masoor*) to the dough mix before the puri are rolled out. Reduce the flour quantity to 6 oz (175 g). Follow the recipe above.

Alu Dolma Puri

POTATO-STUFFED PURI

•

IF ONE has abiding memories of a city it is often its street scenes. Two standard modes of transport in Bangladesh are cycle rickshaws and open, but covered, three-wheeler motorcycle taxis, called *tuk-tuks* in Bangladesh. They seat two passengers who are transported by the driver at great speed and bumpiness through congested streets.

Imagine fairground dodgem cars, then increase the density of traffic and the area of travel by a factor of 1,000. Forget about highway codes, road rage and driving licences. Don't even think about accidents and insurance – just sit back and enjoy the view (or hang on for dear life!). Not that there is much view. Unlike India's *put-puts*, the Bangladeshi version seems to have a lower roof which cuts off one's outward vision to below the waist level of passing pedestrians (most of whom are adept at jumping out of the way of the oncoming tuk-tuk). I became an expert on people's feet and footware. If you bend your head sideways you can see more of the street scene. Halted at more than one traffic jam, we found ourselves within touching distance of roadside snack bars. Their occupants sit lotus-position on a stool, (conveniently thus at bent-neck-view-line) making snacks. One of these is *alu dolma puri*. Ping–pong balls of dough are deftly rolled. A thumb jabs a hole down the centre. The stuffing is inserted. It is hand-slapped into a disc and deep-fried, all in a flash it seems. Just as I was about to make my order, the tuk-tuk would lurch off again to the next traffic jam and next snack bar, so I never got to taste one. Here is my interpretation. Fortunately I don't require you to twist your neck to the horizontal position to make them.

——— MAKES 16 puris ———

8 oz (225 g) wholemeal or ata flour
about 4 tablespoons potato/pea filling (see page 46)

Follow the Loochi recipe opposite to make the puris. At Step 3 make a hole in the ball and add a little stuffing, then cover it before rolling it into a disc and frying.

Moghul Parathas

LAYERED CRISPY BREAD

•

THE *paratha* is a flat, unleavened dough disc about 7–8 inches (18–20 cm) in diameter made, like puff pastry, by thinly rolling and folding over and over to trap air and create layers. The result when pan-fried, should be golden and light, crispy outside, yet soft inside and 'melt-in-the-mouth'. It was a creation of the Moghul emperors.

———— MAKES 4 parathas ————

2 oz (50 g) butter, melted
1 lb (450 g) wholemeal or ata flour, plus extra for flouring
2 tablespoons sultanas

2 tablespoons toasted sliced almonds
½ teaspoon salt
butter ghee or good, light vegetable oil for frying

1. Rub the melted butter into the flour and follow the recipe for unleavened dough on page 142.

2. Divide the dough into four balls, and roll each out into a thin disc. Flour it, then fold it over and over as with puff pastry. Roll out again to a thin disc. Repeat this as many times as you like – the more you do it, the lighter the ultimate texture. Add the sultanas, almonds and salt when you do this for the last time and roll out carefully.

3. Melt the ghee or oil in a frying pan; you will need a depth of about 2 inches (5 cm).

4. Fry the paratha on one side, then the other, to a lovely golden brown colour. Shake off excess oil and drain on kitchen paper. Repeat with the remaining parathas and serve hot.

—— *Variation* ——

Plain paratha Omit the sultanas and almonds.

OPPOSITE Clockwise from top right: *Puishak Chingri* (spinach with shrimp, page 94), *Tarkari Vhaji* (potato and long bean curry, page 154), *Choti* (sweet mango pickle, page 154) and *Panta Bhat* (water rice, page 139). Note the long beans, which can grow up to a metre in length

Bakhar Khani

CHEESE-STUFFED, CRISPY, LAYERED PARATHAS

•

ON OUR visit to Sylhet, Rasheed was very keen to point out the large new houses springing up in the smart parts of the town which are owned by British Bangladeshi restaurateurs. 'Londoni houses' were how he described them: 'Very rich men!' We met several. One, Nizam Ali, was with his young, articulate sisters Rejiya and Sophina. They live in Woking and own three upmarket restaurants including the Jaipur, Tolworth. As we relaxed over a Coke at their lovely Londoni house, their cook appeared with some very English-looking mashed potato and cheese balls. Nizam confided that what he and his sisters miss most on their visits to Bangladesh is English food: 'We especially love Cheddar cheese. In fact, we fill our cases with foodie treats.'

This recipe is therefore dedicated to Nizam, Reji and Sophina, and to all those Bangladeshi Londoni's who miss their Cheddar. By using Cheddar instead of paneer, and white flour, the recipe is an adaptation of one by Sanir Uddin, chef to the former nawabs of Dhaka, who served it at Amin Ali's London Red Fort Restaurant Bangladeshi Food Festival.

——— MAKES 4 parathas ———

2 oz (50 g) butter, melted
1 lb (450 g) strong white flour, plus extra for flouring

4 oz (110 g) grated Cheddar cheese
butter ghee or good, light vegetable oil for frying

1. Rub the melted butter into the flour and follow the recipe for unleavened dough on page 142.

2. Divide the dough into four balls, and roll each out into a thin disc. Flour it, then fold it over and over as with puff pastry. Roll out again to a thin disc. Repeat this as many times as you like – the more you do it, the lighter the ultimate texture. Add the grated Cheddar cheese when you do this for the last time and roll out carefully.

3. Melt the ghee or oil in a frying pan; you will need a depth of about 2 inches (5 cm).

4. Fry the paratha on one side, then the other, to a golden brown. Drain on kitchen paper. Repeat with the remaining parathas and serve hot.

OPPOSITE Top to bottom: *Patishapta Pitha* (crêpes filled with sweet cheese, page 162) served with a small bowl of date palm syrup, and *Rosmalai* (sweet balls in cream, page 161)

CHAPTER 9

ACCOMPANIMENTS

IN THIS short chapter are the items which, for want of a better word, we call accompaniments. They are actually indispensable to a Bangladeshi, being chutneys or pickles.

Chutneys are either an assembly of fresh ingredients, or they are cooked without oil to produce sugar-based preserves such as sweet mango chutney. Pickles, on the other hand, can be raw ingredients steeped in vinegar, which preserves them, but are usually cooked in oil.

The simplest chutney is plain yoghurt just dolloped on the plate. The most complex pickle can take hours to cook and weeks to mature.

A range of bottled mango chutneys and pickles can be readily purchased. These include standard pickled mangos, aubergines, limes and chillies – and very good they are too.

In this chapter I include recipes for making three typical Bangladeshi pickles, none of which is available in the shops. *Amla achar* involves a kind of large olive, *choti* is a sweet mango pickle, and *amb achar* is a sour version.

Also in this chapter are some unusual fresh chutneys.

Begoom Bhoortha

PURÉED VEGETABLE CHUTNEY

•

BHOORTHA or *borta* is a particularly Bangladeshi dish and a main course should rarely be taken without one. One type is a freshly cooked mash or purée of a soft vegetable, to which are added chillies and stir-fried spices. *Korola* bhoortha on page 112 is an example, and using that recipe you could make alternative versions with tomato, any gourd, raw cabbage, white radish, celery, etc. The other type of bhoortha requires no cooking.

This recipe uses cooked aubergine/egg plant (*begoom*) but some other popular versions are potato (*alu bhoortha*), okra (*derosh bhoortha*), cabbage leaf (*bhanda kopee*), shrimp (*chingri bhoortha*) and fish (*maachli bhoortha*).

——— SERVES 4 ———

2×6 inch (15 cm) black aubergines
2 tablespoons mustard blend oil
1 teaspoon Panch Foran (see page 36)
½ teaspoon dry red chilli seeds

1–2 fresh green chillies, sliced
1 tablespoon chopped fresh coriander leaves
4 tablespoons yoghurt (optional)
salt to taste

1. Pre-heat the oven to 350°F/180°C/Gas Mark 4.

2. Make a small slit in each aubergine (to allow the release of steam and prevent bursting) then put them into the oven for at least 30 minutes. They should not burn: they should look wrinkled and darker.

3. Let the aubergines cool, then scoop the flesh out into a mixing bowl, discarding the skin, and mash with a fork.

4. Heat the oil in a karahi or wok. Stir-fry the panch foran and chilli seeds for 30 seconds. Add the chillies and chopped coriander leaves and stir-fry for a couple of minutes more.

5. Put the fried items into the mixing bowl with the aubergine mash. Add the yoghurt if liked and salt to taste. Allow to cool.

6. Chill in the fridge and serve cold.

Bangladeshi Garnish

·

EVERYWHERE we went in Bangladesh we found what looked like the same salad. Made with cucumber, lime wedges and green chilli, it had good colour co-ordination. The cucumbers were always peeled and ribbed longways then thinly sliced, the lime wedges were thinly cut longways, with all pith removed. The chillies were de-stalked, opened out and de-seeded, thus being presented flattened.

We decided this attractive presentation should be called Bangladeshi Garnish, and it appears as an accompaniment in a number of recipes in this book, especially in the second chapter.

—— SERVES 4 ——

8–12 thin slices of cucumber
1 large green lime, cut into 8 wedges
2–4 fresh green chillies

1. Prepare the ingredients as described above.

2. Arrange them decoratively on a side plate. Serve chilled.

Morichi Dhana Sag

GREEN CHILLI AND CORIANDER LEAF RELISH

•

WE MET Dhaka restaurateur Abu Alam earlier. This simple but effective green chilli chutney was his invention and is truly adorable, a real relish. Make it, if possible, a couple of hours ahead to allow it to 'marinate'. It will keep overnight but its bright green colour darkens somewhat.

———— MAKES enough for 4 ————

4 fresh green cayenne chillies, chopped
3 tablespoons chopped fresh coriander leaves
2 tablespoons white distilled malt vinegar

1 teaspoon sugar
⅓ teaspoon salt

Ideally the ingredients should be mashed together in a mortar and pestle – go on it won't kill you – to get a fine purée. The lazy can use a food processor/blender. The chutney should be quite runny and you may need a wee bit of water to help it.

Podina Dhana Sag

MINT AND CORIANDER RELISH

•

THIS is really a variation on the previous recipe, though it is much more traditionally encountered. It is best fresh though it will keep overnight in the fridge.

———— MAKES enough for 4 ————

3 tablespoons chopped fresh mint leaves
3 tablespoons chopped fresh coriander leaves
1 garlic clove, chopped
1 teaspoon Tamarind Purée (see page 38)
   or 1 tablespoon white distilled malt
   vinegar

1 teaspoon sugar
⅓ teaspoon salt

Follow the previous recipe, but please note that you will need a little water to achieve the lightly runny texture required for this one.

Amla Achar

BENGALI OLIVE PICKLE

•

THIS is a fully fledged pickle which uses *amla*, a kind of large sour olive, about $2\frac{1}{2}$ inches (6.5 cm) in size. It is usually available from Asian stores and is worth asking for. If necessary, use good quality green olives with stones, though the taste is different.

This recipe involves a relatively long process as the finished pickle should be allowed to mature in an ample quantity of oil for a few weeks before it is used. Consequently, it makes enough pickle for many helpings.

———— MAKES enough for many helpings ————

2 lb 3 oz (1 kg) amla or green olives
1 tablespoon salt
1 teaspoon turmeric
1 teaspoon chilli powder
6 fl oz (175 ml) vegetable oil
2 teaspoons Panch Foran (see page 36)
10–12 garlic cloves, very finely chopped
4 oz (110 g) dried onion flakes

4 tablespoons bottled curry paste (see page 26)
4–6 fresh green chillies, slit
5 fl oz (150 ml) vinegar, any type
2 tablespoons sugar
1 tablespoon salt

1. Gash the amla and blanch them in boiling water for 3–4 minutes. Drain and dry them, and cut away some of their flesh, spreading out it and the stones on an oven tray. (If using olives, omit the blanch and just gash them.)

2. Mix the salt, turmeric and chilli powder and sprinkle over the amla. Leave them, covered, overnight.

3. Next day, pre-heat the oven to 375°F/190°C/Gas Mark 5.

4. Heat 4 tablespoons of the oil in a lidded casserole dish. Stir-fry the panch foran for 30 seconds. Add the garlic cloves and stir-fry them for 1 minute. Add the onion flakes and curry paste and stir-fry for a further 30 seconds.

5. Add the amla with their stones, chillies, vinegar, sugar and salt and stir-fry until sizzling. Add the remaining oil.

6. Transfer the dish (with lid on) to the oven and cook for 40 minutes. Inspect midway (after 20 minutes) and stir to ensure it is not drying up. In the unlikely event that it is, add just enough water to prevent this.

7. Remove from the oven and allow to become cool enough for bottling.

8. Wash some jam jars and dry them thoroughly in a warming drawer or very low oven.

9. When the pickle is cool enough, transfer it to the jars, filling them to the top and ensuring that there is sufficient oil in each jar. Cap the jars and shake the pickle down.

10. Inspect the jars after a couple of days, ensuring that there is at least $\frac{1}{2}$ inch (1.25 cm) oil above the pickle to prevent it moulding on top. If not, heat some more oil and pour it in.

11. Leave for at least a month before serving.

Amb Achar

TART HOT MANGO PICKLE

•

THIS variation on the previous recipe uses cooking mangos. These are not the luscious, juicy, yellow sweet ones – they appear in the next recipe. Cooking mangos are green and sour and are grown especially for pickle-making. As with the previous recipe, *amb achar* should mature for several weeks before being used.

——— **MAKES enough for several helpings** ———

substitute 2 lb 3 oz (1 kg) sour green pickling mangos for the amla

Follow the recipe for Amla Achar (opposite) in its entirety.

Choti

SWEET MANGO PICKLE

•

I CAME across *Choti* first at a friend's house in Sylhet where it is also known as *murraba*.

Choti is sweet with a hint of sour (from tamarind) and is very mature and dark in colour, the result, I'm told, of hours of Bangladeshi sunshine beating down on both the uncooked mango (at Step 1) and on the finished bottled product. As Bangladeshis in Britain know only too well, there isn't enough sunshine in the United Kingdom, apart from freak summers, so we must omit this step. Nevertheless this recipe creates a good choti, and I'm sure it will liven your palate up at any time. The cooked bottled chutney will keep indefinitely, improving in flavour over time.

—— MAKES ample choti ——

2 lb (900 g) sweet mangos, preferably slightly under-ripe, weighed after de-stoning
1 lb (450 g) molasses sugar
8 garlic cloves, very finely chopped
2–4 fresh red chillies, chopped
2 tablespoons Tamarind Purée (see page 38)

SPICES
2–3 bay leaves
2×2 inch (5 cm) pieces cassia bark
10 cloves
4 green cardamom pods, crushed

1. Wash the mangos, then cut the flesh away from the stones in large chunks. Scrape as much flesh off the stones as you can and set it aside.

2. Bring 10 fl oz (300 ml) water to the boil. Add the mango stones and **spices** and simmer for 20 minutes. Discard the solids but keep the water on the simmer.

3. Add the molasses and dissolve it completely, stirring all the time.

4. Add the mango flesh and the remaining ingredients, and bring to the boil.

5. Immediately lower the heat to achieve a gentle rolling simmer. At first the mixture seems very watery, as the mango flesh turns to pulp, but it quickly reduces and begins to caramelise. It is cooked after about 20 minutes when it will have set to a solid syrupy texture. During the 20 minutes, inspect and stir three or four times.

6. Remove the pan from the heat and let it cool sufficiently to bottle in sterilised jars.

CHAPTER 10

SWEETS

BANGLADESH is famous for its sweets and sweetmeats, harking back to the days when it was part of Bengal. First written evidence comes from as early as 1406, when a Chinese trader, Mahuan, mentioned that he exported sweet candied preserved fruit from Bengal.

We know that by the sixteenth century *halva* (toffee), *burfis* (fudge), sweet yoghurt (*mishti doi*), rice pudding (*payesh*) and the celebrated *jalebi* (spirals of deep-fried batter in syrup), were just a few favourites established in the area.

The biggest breakthrough was yet to come. It was the separation of milk liquids (whey) from their solids (curds) to create cheese. Called *chhana* in Bengal and *paneer* elsewhere in India, it must not be confused with *chana* or Bengal gram (lentil or flour). Introducing a little acid to milk separates it. It was a European concept – all our cheeses stem from the process. It was brought to India in the seventeenth century. Bengal's sweetmakers (*moiras*) took to chhana as ducks to water, using it as a new ingredient for sweetmeats.

In 1868, the 22-year-old Nobin Chandra Das invented the *rosgolla*, a chhana ball cooked in syrup. In 1920 his son, K.C. Das invented the *rasmolai* – a variation of his father's recipe in which the chhana balls are cooked in sweetened milk. Further inventions included the *gulab jaman*, where the ball is deep-fried to golden then immersed in syrup, the *kala jaman* – an egg-shaped variant deep-fried to dark brown – and the *cham cham*, a flattened oval (sometimes boat-shaped) variant fried golden or brown and immersed in syrup, then sprinkled with *khoa* (dried milk powder). Das went on to open a factory, still extant, to mass-produce (and can) such sweetmeats, and his descendants run Calcutta's most famous sweet shop, K.C. Das on Esplanade Road. Many more shapes and variants were invented and the most notable was dedicated to Lady Canning, wife of Britain's first viceroy of India. Now known as *ledikeni*, it is a mango-shaped cham cham.

There are now said to be thousands of sweets. Here are just some of them.

Mishti Doi

SWEETENED YOGHURT

•

STARTING with the easiest first, here is a simple and effective dessert.

—— SERVES 4 ——

1 lb (450 g) home-made yoghurt (see page 33) or Greek-style yoghurt
2–3 tablespoons golden syrup
½ teaspoon ground cardamom seeds
10–15 saffron strands (optional)

GARNISH
freshly grated nutmeg
chopped pistachio nuts

1. Whisk the ingredients together.

2. Let the mixture stand in the fridge for an hour or more to allow the saffron strands, if used, to 'exude' their flavour and colour. It will actually be safe in the fridge until the yoghurt's use-by date.

3. Put into stemmed glasses, garnish with the nutmeg and pistachio nuts, and serve.

—— *Variation* ——

Mishti Doi can be served as a *lhassi*-style drink. To serve four, add 8 fl oz (225 ml) water to the ingredients. Omit the garnish and serve the drink in tall glasses with crushed ice.

Paesh

SPICY RICE PUDDING

•

SOMEHOW rice pudding still has connotations with bad school dinners. Yet it is quite delicious, if done properly, and more especially so if it is spiced the Bangladeshi way. In this ultra-quick version you can let someone else do the hard work by using tinned creamed rice. It can be served hot, but serving it cold seems to bring out the flavours more.

──────── SERVES 4 ────────

14 oz (400 g) tinned creamed rice
10–15 saffron strands
1 tablespoon sugar

$\frac{1}{2}$ teaspoon ground cardamom seeds
freshly grated nutmeg to garnish

Simply mix the ingredients and allow them to stand for at least an hour while the saffron infuses. Garnish with the nutmeg. Serve hot or cold.

Chhana

SOFT COTTAGE CHEESE

•

I MENTIONED earlier how certain sweets evolved. First you must make *chhana* (or soft *paneer*). It's easy.

The *moiras* (Bengali sweetmakers) actually use whey (from a previous batch of chhana) to cause the separation. They claim it creates softer (less granular) curds. If you have some retained whey, use it. Fresh lemon juice is the next best acidic medium. Don't, they implore, use vinegar: it's too harsh.

——— MAKES about 8 oz (225 g) ———

4 pints (2.25 litres) full cream milk (not UHT)
4–6 tablespoons lemon juice

1. Choose a large pan. If you have one of 12 pint (6.75 litre) capacity, the milk will only occupy one-third and won't boil over (unless the lid is on).

2. Bring the milk slowly to the boil. Add the lemon juice, stirring until the milk curdles — when the curds separate from the whey.

3. Strain through muslin or a clean tea towel placed on a sieve over a saucepan or bowl. Fold the tea towel over and press the excess liquid — the whey — through. Keep for later use as stock.

4. Now place the curds — now called chhana — on the draining board, still in the tea towel. Press out to a circle about $\frac{1}{2}$ inch (1 cm) thick. Place a flat weight (the original saucepan full of water, for instance) on the tea towel and allow it to compress the chhana.

5. Remove the weight after 30–45 minutes and crumble the chhana.

Rosgolla

CAKE-LIKE BALLS IN SUGAR SYRUP

•

Ros means juice and *golla* round, and that's what Mr Das chose to call his invention – juicy balls! Notice I have refrained from calling them 'cheese' balls in the translation, but that's what they are; *chhana* is moulded to small balls which are then simmered in syrup. Left to cool in the fridge overnight, when they swell a little and become light, they absorb syrup and are a best-seller. So say the Das family. Here's the secret.

——— MAKES 8 large or 12 smaller rosgollas ———

8 oz (225 g) chhana curds (see opposite)
up to 3 tablespoons plain white flour

2 lb (900 g) white sugar
2–3 tablespoons rosewater to serve

1. Knead the chhana in a bowl with just enough flour and water to create a smooth, pliable dough.

2. Divide the dough into 8–12 equal-sized pieces, then roll these into balls.

3. In a large saucepan, make the syrup by bringing 2 pints (1.2 litres) water to the boil and adding the sugar. Dissolve it completely – the syrup will be quite thin – then maintain a simmer.

4. Add the balls one at a time and simmer them for 20 minutes, ensuring, particularly early on, that they do not stick together. The syrup should not become too thick. If it starts to, add a little water.

5. By the end of the 20 minutes, the rosgollas should all be enlarged a little, and light enough to float. The syrup should be a little thicker.

6. Remove from the heat. Transfer to a non-metallic bowl. Cool, then cover and keep overnight in the fridge.

7. Just prior to serving, sprinkle rosewater over the rosgollas. Serve cold.

Gulab Jamun

GOLDEN GLOBES IN SYRUP

•

GULAB JAMUN means a rosy plum, a reference to its shape, and this sweetmeat is my wife Dominique's favourite, especially when it is served still warm, flambéed with brandy for a special occasion – to follow the lobster on page 108 and accompanied by pink champagne, perhaps. (To achieve a flambé, ensure the warm balls are not swamped in the syrup.)

The *chhana* is moulded to plum shapes (though they can be round) and fried to a golden colour before being steeped in saffron-enhanced syrup. Gulab jamun are commonly found at the better curry restaurants – though they are never as good as when they are home-made!

———— MAKES 8 gulab jamun ————

8 oz (225 g) chhana curds (see page 158)	2 lb (900 g) white sugar
up to 3 tablespoons plain white flour	20–25 saffron strands
vegetable oil for deep-frying	2–3 tablespoons rosewater to serve

1. Knead the chhana in a bowl with just enough flour and water to create a smooth, pliable dough.

2. Divide the dough to make eight chhana balls and mould them to plum shapes.

3. In a deep-fryer heat the oil to 375°F/190°C, then add the 'balls' one at a time, to maintain the oil temperature, and fry until they become quite golden, but not brown (about 2–3 minutes).

4. Meanwhile, make the syrup then add the hot fried balls and simmer them in the syrup for 18–20 minutes (see Steps 3 and 4 of the previous recipe).

5. Add the saffron and follow the previous recipe to its end. Serve warm, at the end of cooking, or cold.

Cham Cham

GOLDEN BOAT-SHAPED BALLS

•

A SHAPE variant of *gulab jamun*. They can be flattened discs or boat shaped, and are served without syrup. The traditional garnish is *khoa*, milk reduced until it becomes a powder. As it takes a day of non-stop stirring to produce a cupful of khoa, use factory-made milk powder, or ground almonds.

——— **MAKES 6 cham cham** ———

Follow the previous Gulab Jamun recipe. Simply divide the dough into six portions and shape them into boats (or flattened, rissole-shaped discs).

Remove from the syrup (which can be saved for other uses). Garnish with milk powder or ground almonds and serve chilled.

Rosmolai

SWEET BALLS IN CREAM

•

Mr das Junior took 50 years to find this variation on his father's *rosgolla* (see chapter introduction). Luckily, you won't have to wait that long. I think *rosmolai* (*molai* means cream) are nicer even than rosgolla, especially when the balls are miniature ones (acorn-size and shape) as you'll find at Dhaka's Sonargaon hotel's Jharna restaurant.

——— **MAKES 16–24 rosmolai** ———

8 oz (225 g) chhana curds (see page 158)	7 fl oz (200 ml) single cream
up to 3 tablespoons plain white flour	3½ fl oz (100 ml) evaporated milk
2 lb (900 g) white sugar	2 tablespoons sugar
2–3 tablespoons rosewater	½ teaspoon ground cardamom seeds

1. Knead the chhana in a bowl with just enough flour and water to create a smooth, pliable dough. Divide the dough to make 16–24 acorn shapes.

2. Make the syrup and simmer the 'acorns' as in the recipe on page 159. Add the rosewater.

3. Remove the rosmolai from the syrup when cold. Keep the syrup for another time.

4. In a non-stick saucepan bring the cream, evaporated milk, sugar and cardamom to just under the simmer. Try not to boil it. Take it off the heat then put the rosmolai into the cream. When cold, cover and keep in the fridge overnight. Serve cold.

Patishapta Pitha

CRÊPES FILLED WITH SWEET CHEESE

•

*P*ITHA is Bangladeshi for sweets which use thickened milk (as opposed to *chhana*) or pastry. Chef Gomes tells me he knows of over 500 recipes for them! This pitha is particularly nice. A white crêpe is filled with thickened milk (cheesecake mixture in this case). It was served, with some flourish, at the Dhaka Sheraton hotel's Bithika restaurant, accompanied by a small jug of dark brown, warm, date palm syrup. Real maple syrup is a substitute.

As this dish is particularly rich, I suggest you make only four pancakes. The batter mixture will make more because I find that the first one never works! Pancakes can be cooked in advance, stored between layers of foil and refrigerated for a day or frozen.

──── SERVES 4 ────

2 oz (50 g) plain white flour
1 oz (25 g) butter, melted, plus extra for
    cooking
1 egg, beaten
5 fl oz (150 ml) milk, warmed
1 teaspoon sugar
2–3 drops vanilla essence
maple syrup, and lime wedges to serve

FILLING

4 oz (110 g) soft cream cheese
2 oz (50 g) thick soured cream
1 teaspoon sugar
$\frac{1}{2}$ teaspoon ground cardamom seeds
$\frac{1}{4}$ teaspoon freshly grated nutmeg

GARNISH
icing sugar
freshly grated nutmeg

1. Sift the flour into a bowl and mix in the butter, egg, warm milk, sugar and vanilla. Beat well and leave to stand for about 10 minutes. It should be of pouring consistency. In a very hot omelette or griddle pan, heat a little butter. Pour in enough batter to make a thin pancake when 'swirled' around the pan. Cook until set, then turn over and briefly cook the other side. Turn out. Repeat with the remaining batter. Allow the pancakes to go cold.

2. Mix the filling ingredients together and mash until smooth.

3. Spread one-quarter of the filling across the centre line of one pancake. Roll the pancake into a cylinder. Repeat with the other three pancakes.

4. Warm the maple syrup. Dust the cold pancakes with icing sugar and nutmeg and serve with the warm syrup and lime wedges.

Chaal Kumra Pitha

WHITE PUMPKIN SWEET PRESERVE

•

WE MET Professor Shafique at his tea plantation bungalow on page 53. It is apt that he has the last word (in the recipe introductions, at any rate). His cook produced this sumptuous white pumpkin sweet preserve in syrup. It is a translucent gold colour, punctuated by the brown of cassia bark. *Chaal kumra pitha* will keep for several days in the fridge, so this recipe makes enough for more than one nibble.

As we nibbled the sweet, Professor Shafique pointed to the horizon, a truly beautiful view of lush trees and shrubs as far as the eye could see. A monkey flashed by. 'We are learning not to cut the forest away,' he said. 'We plant new trees now. And under them we must ensure the shrubs return. Shrubs give cover to our animals and birds. Even the monkey needs privacy.'

1 lb (450 g) white or yellow pumpkin	1 lb (450 g) sugar
several small pieces cassia bark	20–30 saffron strands

1. Peel the pumpkin. Remove the seeds and pith. Cut the flesh into $1\frac{1}{2}$ inch (3.75 cm) cubes. Blanch them to soften.

2. In a non-stick saucepan, bring 1 pint (600 ml) water to the boil with the cassia bark. Add the sugar and stir until it dissolves.

3. Add the pumpkin cubes and saffron to the syrup and, on a very low heat, simmer for about 30–40 minutes. The syrup should be thicker by now and most will have been absorbed into the pumpkin, making it translucent.

4. Place the cubes on foil and let them cool.

APPENDIX I

THE CURRY CLUB

Pat Chapman always had a deep-rooted interest in spicy food, curry in particular, and over the years he built up a huge pool of information which he felt could be usefully passed on to others. He conceived the idea of forming an organisation for this purpose.

Since it was founded in January 1982, **The Curry Club** has built up a membership of several thousands. We have a marchioness, some lords and ladies, knights a-plenty, a captain of industry or two, generals, admirals and air marshals (not to mention a sprinkling of ex-colonels), and we have celebrity names – actresses, politicians, rock stars and sportsmen. We have an airline (Air India), a former Royal Navy warship (HMS *Hermes*) and a hotel chain (the Taj group).

We have 15 members whose name is Curry or Currie, 20 called Rice and several with the name Spice or Spicer, Cook, Fry, Frier or Fryer and one Boiling. We have a Puri (a restaurant owner), a Paratha and a Nan and a good many Mills and Millers, one Dal and a Lentil, an Oiler, a Gee (but no Ghee), and a Butter but no Marj (several Marjories though, and a Marjoram and a Minty). We also have several Longs and Shorts, Thins and Broads, one Fatt and one Wide, and a Chilley and a Coole.

We have members on every continent including a good number of Asian members, but by and large the membership is a typical cross-section of the Great British Public, ranging in age from teenage to dotage, and in occupation from refuse collectors to receivers, high street traders to high court judges, tax inspectors to taxi drivers. There are students and pensioners, millionaires and unemployed ... thousands of people who have just one thing in common – a love of curry and spicy foods.

Members receive a bright and colourful quarterly magazine which has regular features on curry and the curry lands. It includes news items, recipes, reports on restaurants, picture features, and contributions from members and professionals alike. The information is largely concerned with curry, but by popular demand it now includes regular input on other exotic and spicy cuisines such as those of the Middle East and China. We produce a wide selection of publications, including the books listed on page ii, all published by Piatkus.

Obtaining some of the ingredients required for curry cooking can be difficult, but The Curry Club makes it easy, with a comprehensive range of Curry Club products, including spice mixes, chutneys, pickles, papadoms, sauces and curry pastes. These are available from major food stores and specialist delicatessens up and down the country. If they are not stocked near you, there is the Club's well-established and efficient mail-order service. Hundreds of items are stocked, including spices, pickles, pastes, dry foods, tinned foods, gift items, publications and specialist kitchen and tableware.

On the social side, the Club holds residential weekend cookery courses and gourmet nights at selected restaurants. Top of the list is our regular Curry Club gourmet trip to India and other spicy countries. We take a small group of curry enthusiasts to the chosen country and tour the incredible sights, in between sampling the delicious foods of each region.

If you would like more information about The Curry Club, write (enclosing a stamped addressed envelope please) to: **The Curry Club, PO Box 7, Haslemere, Surrey GU27 1EP.**

APPENDIX 2

THE STORE CUPBOARD

THE ITEMS listed include the spices and specialist non-perishable ingredients needed to make the recipes in this book. I have not given quantities because they vary from manufacturer to manufacturer.

The items marked ★ are used in one or, at most, just a few recipes. The others are frequently called for.

All items listed are available by post from The Curry Club, see Appendix 1.

Whole Spices

Aniseed★ (*saunf*)
Bay Leaves (*tej pattia*)
Cardamom, black or brown (*burra elaichi*)
Cardamom, green or white (*elaichi*)
Cassia Bark (*dalchini chino*)
Celery Seeds (*celo dorroo*)
Chillies, red dry (*lal mirch*)
Cinnamon Quill★ (*dalchini*)
Cloves (*lavang*)
Coriander Seeds (*dhania*)
Coriander Seeds, tiny★ (*chotaswaz*)
Cummin Seeds, black (*kala jeera*)

Cummin Seeds, white (*jeera*)
Curry Leaves, dry (*neem pattia*)
Fenugreek Leaves, dry (*methi pattia*)
Fenugreek Seeds (*methi*)
Lovage Seeds (*ajwain*)
Mace (*javitri*)
Mustard Seeds, black (*rai*)
Nutmeg, whole (*jaifal*)
Peppercorns, black (*mirch*)
Poppy Seeds, white (*cuscus*)
Saffron Stamens (*zafran*)
Sesame Seeds, white (*til*)
Wild Onion Seeds (*kalongi*)

Ground Spices

Asafoetida★ (*hing*)
Cardamom★ (*elaichi*)
Chilli (*lal mirch*)
Cinnamon (*dalchini*)
Clove (*lavang*)
Coriander (*dhania*)
Cummin (*jeera*)
Curry Powder★
Mango Powder★
Mustard Powder, yellow★
Paprika
Pepper, black
Pepper, white
Turmeric (*haldi*)

Non-Perishable Foods

Basmati rice
Chupatti flour (*ata*)
Coconut,
 desiccated
 milk powder
 tinned
Curry Paste, bottled★

Gram flour
 Bengal gram★ (*chana dal*)
 Green split peas★ (*motor shut*)
 Red lentils, split and polished★ (*masoor
 dal*)
 Yellow split peas★ (*motor dal*)
Mango Chutney, sweet bottled
Nuts
 Almonds,
 ground
 sliced
 whole
 Cashews
 Pistachio
Onion Flakes, dried★
Oils
 Mustard Blend Oil
 Sunflower Oil
 Vegetable Oil
Papadoms,
 spiced
 plain (pack)
Rosewater, bottle★
Tamarind, block
Tandoori (curry) paste, bottle★

GLOSSARY

THIS GLOSSARY is very extensive, including some items not specifically mentioned in the recipes. It is intended to be used as a general reference work. If you do not find a particular word here it is worth checking to see whether it is in the index and can be found elsewhere in the book.

The principal language in Bangladesh is Bengali (one of India's 15 languages), although there are dialects and even major differences from place to place, e.g. Sylhet.

The English spelling is 'standard' but can vary as words are translated phonetically.

A

achar – pickle

ada – ginger

ajwain or ajowain – lovage seeds

alu – potato

akhni – spicy consommé-like liquid stock

amb – mango

ambal – sweet and sour

am chur – mango powder

amla – sour olive type vegetable

amli – tamarind

anarosh – pineapple

anday – egg

angur – grape

aniseed – *saunf*. Small deliciously flavoured seeds resembling fennel seeds

asafoetida – *hing*. A rather smelly spice

ata or atta – *chupatti* flour. Fine wholemeal flour used in most Indian breads. English wholemeal is a suitable alternative

B

Badain – star anise

badam – almond

bagda – king prawns (12–15 per lb)

bahn morog – red jungle fowl

banda kopee – cabbage

bang – frog-leg

barbati – red kidney bean

bargar – the process of frying whole spices in hot oil

basmati – the best type of long-grain rice

bati or bhera bati – lamb

bati – serving bowl

bayam – eel

bay leaf – *tej pattia*. Aromatic spice

besan – See *gram flour*

begoom (begum) – aubergine

bekti – large white fish

bhaja – fried

bhajee or bhaji – dryish mild vegetable curry

bhajia – deep-fried fritter, usually onion. Same as *pakora*

bhare – stuffed

bharta or bhurta – mash or purée

bhat – rice

bhera – sheep/mutton

bhoona or bhuna – the process of cooking the spice paste in hot oil. A *bhoona* curry is usually dry and cooked in coconut

bhoortha (borta) – puréed or shredded items

bhija – wet

bhutta – maize

bilati begoom – tomato

bilati motor – pea**

biriani – rice cooked with meat/poultry/vegetables originated in Iran and taken to Bangladesh by the Moghuls

boal – round white fish

borof – ice

borofer pani – iced water

bursunga – curry leaf

C

cardamom – *elaichi*. One of the most aromatic and expensive spices

cashew nuts – *kaju*

cassia bark – aromatic spice, related to cinnamon

cayenne pepper – a blend of chilli powder from Latin America

Ceylon curry – usually cooked with coconut, lemon and chilli

chagaler mansa – mutton

chagol – goat

chaku (churi) – knife

chamoch – spoon

chara – plant

charchuri (chach chori) – a curry cooking process

chaul – rice

chhana paneer (soft cheese)

chichinga – snake gourd

chingri/chingri maach – prawns

chini – sugar

chola – gram lentil (chana)

chotaswaz – tiny coriander seeds

choti – sweet mango pickle

chula – brick stove lined with mud or dung

Chupatti – a dry 6 inch (15 cm) disc of unleavened bread. Normally griddle-cooked, it should be served piping hot. Spelling varies, e.g. *Chupati, Chapati,* etc.

chutneys – the common ones are onion, mango and tandoori. There are dozens of others which rarely appear on the standard menu

cinnamon – *dalchini*. One of the most aromatic spices

cloves – *lavang*. Expensive and fragrant spice

coriander – *dhania*. One of the most important spices in curry cookery. The leaves of the plant can be used fresh and the seeds whole or ground

cummin or cumin – *jeera*. There are two types of seeds: *white* and *black*. The white seeds are a very important spice in Indian cookery. The black seeds (*kala jeera*) are nice in pullao rice and certain vegetable dishes. Both can be used whole or ground

curry – the only word in this glossary to have no direct translation into any of the subcontinent's 15 or so languages. The word was coined by the British in India centuries ago. Possible contenders for the origin of the word are: *karahi* or *karai* (Hindi), a wok-like frying pan used all over India to prepare masalas (spice mixtures); *kurhi*, a soup-like dish made with spices, gram flour dumplings and buttermilk; *kari*, a spicy Tamil sauce; *turkuri*, a seasoned sauce or stew; *kari phulia, neem* or curry leaves; *kudhi* or *kadhi*, a yoghurt soup; or *koresh*, an aromatic Iranian stew

curry lands – India is the main curry land with 800 million, mainly Hindu, people. Other curry lands are her Moslem neighbours to the west – Pakistan, Afghanistan, and, to a lesser extent, Iran which is the root of some Indian food. To the north lie Nepal and Bhutan whilst Moslem Bangladesh lies to the east. India's south-eastern curry-land neighbours include the predominantly Buddhist Burma and Thailand, whilst multinational Malaysia and Singapore, with huge, mainly Moslem Indian populations, are also curry lands. The tiny island of Sri Lanka has a very distinctive curry style and one must not forget significant pockets of curry-eating Asians in Africa and the Caribbean. The total number of people whose 'staple' diet is curry exceeds 1 billion people – 25 per cent of the world's population

curry leaves – *neem* leaves or *kari phulia*. Small leaves a bit like bay leaves, used for flavouring

cus cus – see *poppy seed*

D

dhal – or lentils. There are over 60 types of lentil in the subcontinent, some of which are very obscure. Like peas, they grow into a hard sphere measuring between $\frac{1}{2}$ inch (1 cm) (chickpeas) and $\frac{1}{8}$ inch (3 mm) (urid). They are cooked whole or split with skin, or split with the skin polished off. Lentils are a rich source of protein and when cooked with spices are extremely tasty. The common types are:

Bengal gram (*chana* in Hindi) – *chola* or *gota*; Chick peas – *kobuli chola* Black Lentils (*urid* in Hindi) – *Mashkalai*; Green Lentils (*moong* in Hindi) – *mug*; Red Lentils (*masoor* in Hindi) – *masuri*; Green Peas (dried), *atar* – *sukhna motor*; Red Kidney Beans (*rajmah* in Hindi) – *razma* or *barbati*; Yellow split peas – *motor dal*

dalchini or darchim – Cinnamon

dalna – fried vegetable curry with a little sweetener

dana-zira – see pages 69 and 98. A spice mix composed mainly of coriander and cummin

derosh – okra/ladies' fingers

dhana sag – coriander leaf

dhania – coriander

dhansak – traditional Parsee dish cooked in a purée of lentils, aubergine, tomato and spinach. Some restaurants also add pineapple pieces

dheki (decchi) – waisted cooking utensil

dim – egg

dim bhaja – fried egg/omelette

doi – yoghurt

dolma – stuffed vegetable

dom – steam cooking. Long before the West invented the pressure cooker, India had her own method which lasts to this day. A pot with a close-fitting lid is sealed with a ring of dough. The ingredients are then cooked in their own steam under some pressure

doomur – peach

dopeyaja – curry with plentiful onion. *Do* means two and *peyaja* means onion. It gets its name because onions appear twice in the cooking process

E

elaichi – cardamom

F

fennel – *sunf* or *soonf*. A small green seed which is very aromatic, with aniseed taste

fenugreek – *methi*. This important spice is used as seeds and in fresh or dried leaf form. It is very savoury and is used in many northern Indian dishes

fol – fruit

ful – flower

G

gajor – carrot

garlic – *lasan*

ghee – clarified butter or margarine much used in Bangladeshi cookery

ghonto – fish head

ginger – *ada* (fresh), *sont* (dried), a rhizome which can be used fresh, dried or powdered

golda – large prawn (6–8 per lb)

golmorich – pepper

gom – wheat

gorom – hot

gorom masholla (moshalla) – hot mixture of spices (garam masala)

goru – cow

gorur mangsho (go mangse) – beef

gota – gram lentils (chana)

gram flour – *besan*. Finely ground flour, pale blonde in colour, made from chana (see *dhal*). Used to make *pakoras* and to thicken curries

gusht (gosht/gust) – meat

H

halde (holde) – yellow or turmeric

hansha or hash – duck

hilsa – bony fish

hing – asafoetida

horin – venison

J

jal (jhal) – pungently spicy stir-fry

jaifal or taifal – nutmeg

jal frezi – sautéed or stir-fried meat or chicken dish, often with lightly cooked onion, garlic, ginger, green bell pepper and chilli

jalebi – an Indian dessert. A flour, milk powder and yoghurt batter pushed through a narrow funnel into deep-frying oil to produce golden curly crispy rings. Served cold or hot in syrup

javatri – mace

jeera or zeera – cummin

jol (jhol) – water or boiling process

K

kacchu – raw

kacha – unripe

kafi – coffee – grown in Bangladesh

kaju – cashew nut

kakrul – small gourd

kala – banana flesh

kala – black

kala jeera – black cummin seeds

kala namak – black salt

kalia – a curry process, incorporating red colours and poppy seeds

kalongi – See *wild onion seeds*

kanch kala – green banana (plantain)

kankra – crab

kanta – fork

karahi – *karai, korai* etc. The Bangladeshi equivalent of the wok. The *karahi* is a circular two-handled round all-purpose cooking pan used for stir-frying, simmering, frying and deep-frying – in fact it is highly efficient for all types of cooking. Some restaurants cook in small *karahis* and serve them straight to the table with the food sizzling inside

Kashmir curry – restaurateurs' creation. A sweetish curry often using lychees or similar ingredient

kathal – jack fruit

katla – silver carp

katori – small serving bowls which go on a *thali* (tray)

kebab – skewered food cooked over charcoal. A process over 4,000 years old which probably originated in Turkey where 'kebab' means 'cooked meat'. It was imported by the Moslems centuries ago. (See *shami* and *sheek kebabs*)

keema – minced meat curry

kewra – screwpine water. An extract of the flower of the tropical screwpine tree. It is a fragrant clear liquid used to flavour sweets. It is a cheap substitute for rosewater

khaddyo – food

khana (khabar) – meal

khatta – sour

khoa – powdered milk

khurzi – lamb or chicken, whole with spicy stuffing and/or coating, also called *kashi*

kish mish – sultanas
kitchuri – rice cooked with lentils
kobuli chola – chickpea
kocchu – green colocasia leaf
kofta – minced meat or vegetable balls in batter, deep-fried, and then cooked in a curry sauce
kofta – ball, e.g. meatball
kola – banana
kopir – cauliflower
korola – bitter gourd
korma – to most restaurants this just means a mild curry. Traditionally it is very rich. Meat, chicken or vegetables are cooked in cream, yoghurt and nuts, and are fragrantly spiced with saffron and aromatic spices. Actually *korma* is a frying method and it is possible to find very hot *kormas*. Chillies are an optional extra in the Bangladeshi version
kulcha – small leavened bread. It can be stuffed with mildly spiced mashed potato and baked in the tandoor
kulfi – Indian ice cream. Traditionally it comes in vanilla, pistachio or mango flavours
kumra – sweet pumpkin
kus kus – see *poppy seed*

L

lal – red
lalshak (lal shag) – red spinach (amaranth leaf)
lasan – garlic
lavang – cloves
lentils – see *dal*
lobon – salt
lovage – *Ajwain* or *ajowain*. Slightly bitter round seeds

M

maach or maachli – fish
mace – *Javitri*. The outer part of the nutmeg

Madras – you will not find a traditional recipe for Madras curry. It is another restaurateurs' invention. But the people of South India *do* eat hot curries; some original chef must have christened his hot curry 'Madras' and the name stuck
magur – large catfish
mahish – buffalo
makhani – a traditional dish. Tandoori chicken is cooked in a ghee and tomato sauce
Malaya – the curries of Malaya are traditionally cooked with plenty of coconut, chilli and ginger. In the Indian restaurant, however, they are usually mild and contain pineapple and other fruit
mango powder – *am chur*. A very sour flavouring agent
mangsho – meat
makhon (mokhon) – butter
maloyborof – ice cream
marraba/murraba – sweet pickle
mashkalai – black lentils (*urid*)
masuri – red lentils
meat – *gusht* or *mangsho*
  beef – *gorur mangsho (go mangse)*
  buffalo – *mahish*
  cow – *goru*
  goat – *chagol*
  lamb – *bati* or *bhera bati*
  mutton – *chagaler mansa*
  pork – *shukor*
methi – fenugreek
mishti – sweet
mod – wine
mochar – banana flower (edible)
Moghuls (Mugals) – the influential emperors of the fifteenth to eighteenth centuries, controlled Bengal as part of India
Moglai or Moghlai – cooking in the style of the Moghuls whose chefs took Indian cookery to the heights of gourmet. Few restaurateurs who offer Moglai dishes come anywhere near this excellence.

True Moghlai dishes are expensive and time-consuming to prepare authentically. Can also be variously spelt muglai, mogulai, moglai, etc.

mojoj – brain

molai (malai) – cream

morghi (morog) – chicken

morichi – chilli

moshalla – (masala in Hindi). A mixture of spices which are cooked with a particular dish. Any curry powder is therefore a masala. It can be spelt a remarkable number of ways – massala, massalla, musala, mosola, massalam, etc.

motor – pea

motor dal – yellow split pea

mug – green lentils (moong)

mula – raddish

murola – tiny fish, e.g. whitebait

mustard seeds rai – small black seeds which become sweetish when fried

N

narikel – coconut

nigella – wild onion seeds

niramish – vegan vegetable dish

noon – salt

norom panio – soft drink

nutmeg – *jaifal*

O

okra – *derosh*. A pulpy vegetable also known as ladies' fingers

P

paka – ripe

pakan – to bake

pakkara – to roast

pakora – gram flour fritter

pan – betel leaf

panch foran (porch foron, etc.) – five seeds. A mixture of five spices used in Bengali vegetable cooking

pani – water

Papadom – thin lentil flour wafers. When cooked (deep-fried or baked) they expand to about 8 inches (20 cm). They must be crackling crisp and warm when served. If not send them back to be reheated and deduct points from that restaurant. They come plain or spiced with lentils, pepper, garlic or chilli. Many spelling variations include popadom, pappodom, etc.

paprika – mild red ground pepper made from red capsicum peppers. Its main use is to give red colour to a dish

paratha – a deep-fried bread

pasanda – meat, usually lamb, beaten and cooked in one piece

pat – jute

pat shak (patua sag) – jute leaves

peeaz, peyaja or pyaz – onion

pepper – *golmorich or mirch*. Has for centuries been India's most important spice. Peppercorns are a heat agent and can be used whole or ground

pesta – pistachio

phal or phall – a very hot curry (the hottest), invented by Bangladeshi restaurateurs

phul kopee – cauliflower

pickles – pungent, hot pickled vegetables or meat essential to an Indian meal. Most common are lime, mango and chilli

pipasha – thirsty

pitha – pastry/sweet cookie

pistachio nut – *pista magaz*. A fleshy, tasty nut which can be used fresh (the greener the better) or salted. It is expensive and goes well in savoury or sweet dishes such as biriani or pista kulfi (ice cream)

podina – mint

pomfret – flatish fish (silver or black species)

poppy seed – cus cus or kus kus. White seeds used in chicken curries, blue seeds used to decorate bread. (Not to be

confused with the Moroccan national
dish cous-cous, made from steamed
semolina)

posto (poshta) – white poppy seeds

potol (patal/parwal) – small pointed
gourd

pran – heart

prawn butterfly – *jinga prai patia*. Prawn
marinated in spices and fried in batter

prawn puri – prawns in a hot sauce served
on puri bread

puishak – type of spinach leaf

pullao – rice and meat or vegetables
cooked together in a pan until tender. In
many restaurants the ingredients are
mixed after cooking to save time (see
also Biriani)

pullao rice – the restaurant name for rice
fried with spices and coloured yellow

pulses – dried peas and beans, including
lentils

puri – a deep-fried unleavened bread about
4 inches (10 cm) in diameter. It puffs up
when cooked and should be served at
once

pyaz (piyaj) – onion

Q

quas chawal or kesar chaval – rice fried
in ghee, flavoured and coloured with
saffron

R

rai – mustard seeds

raita – a cooling chutney of yoghurt and
vegetable, cucumber for instance, which
accompanies the main meal

ranna ghar – kitchen

rangalu – sweet potato

rashum – garlic

razma – red kidney bean

rezala – a creamier curry than Korma (q.v.)
in which green chillies are mandatory.

rhogan josh or gosht – literally it means

red juice meat, or lamb in red gravy. It
is a traditional northern Indian dish.
Lamb is marinated in yoghurt, then
cooked with ghee, spices and tomato. It
should be creamy and spicy but not too
hot. There are many ways of spelling it:
rogon, roghan, rugon, rugin, rowgen,
ragan, etc; jush, joosh, jesh, etc; goosht,
goose, gost, etc.

rhui (rui/ralw) – large pink fleshed type
of carp. The King of the River

rosewater – *ruh gulab*. A clear essence
extracted from rose petals to give
fragrance to sweets. See *kewra*

rosh – juice

ruh gulab – rosewater essence

ruti – bread

S

saffron – *kesar* or *zafron*. The world's most
expensive spice, used to give a recipe a
delicate yellow colouring and aroma

sag or saag – Spinach

sajina danta – drumstick gourd

samosa – the celebrated triangular deep-
fried meat or vegetable patties served as
starters or snacks

saunf or souf – Aniseed

sep – apple

sesame seed – *til*

shaktora – grapefruit-like vegetable from
Sylhet

shami kebab – round minced meat rissoles

shashlik – cubes of skewered lamb

sheek or seekh kebab – Spiced minced
meat shaped on a skewer and grilled or
barbecued. Also called shish kebab, shish
meaning skewer in Turkish. See *kebab*

shing – small catfish

shobji – vegetable

shorse (sorsi) – mustard

shossa (sasha) – cucumber

shukti (shuktoni) – bitter curry

shukna motor – dried green pea

shukor – pork

shushadu – tasty

sonf – fennel seed

sont or south – dry ginger

star anise – a pretty star-shaped aromatic spice

subcontinent – term to describe India, Pakistan, Bangladesh, Nepal, Burma, and Sri Lanka as a group

supari – mixture of seeds and sweeteners for chewing after a meal. Usually includes aniseed or fennel, shredded betel nut, sugar balls, marrow seeds, etc.

T

taipal or jaiphal – nutmeg

tamarind – *amli*. A date-like fruit used as a chutney, and in cooking as a souring agent

tambakash – flat iron disc, sometimes perforated, with long handle, used in deep-frying

tandoori – a style of charcoal cooking originating in north-west India (what is now Pakistan and the Punjab). Originally it was confined to chicken and lamb (see *boti kebab*) and naan bread. More recently it is applied to lobster, etc. The meat is marinated in a reddened yoghurt sauce and placed in the tandoor

tarka – garnish of spices/onion

tarka dhal – lentils garnished with fried spices

tarkari (torkori) – curry

tava or tawa – a heavy, almost flat, circular wooden-handled griddle pan used to cook Indian breads and to 'roast' spices. Also ideal for many cooking functions from frying eggs and omelettes to making pancakes, etc.

tehari – variety of biriani (q.v.)

tej patia – the leaf of the cassia bark tree. Resembles bay leaf which can be used in its place

temuti – tomato

thala/thali – plate

thali sets – to serve your meal in truly authentic fashion use *thali* sets. A great and stylish talking point. Each diner is served a *thali* tray on which are a number of *katori* dishes in which different curry dishes, rice, chutneys, etc., are placed. Bread and pappadoms go on the tray itself

thora – banana stem (edible)

tikka – skewered meat, chicken or seafood, marinated then barbecued or tandoori baked

til – sesame seed

tindla – a vegetable of the cucumber family

tindaloo – See *vindaloo*

tok (syl) – sour

turmeric – *haldi* or *huldi*. A very important spice, used to give the familiar yellow colour to curries. Use sparingly or it can cause bitterness

V

vaji or vhaji – see *bhaji*

vark or varak – edible silver or gold foil

vindaloo – a fiery hot dish from Goa. Traditionally it was pork marinated in vinegar with potato (*aloo*). In the restaurant it has now come to mean just a very hot dish. Also sometimes called *bindaloo* or *tindaloo* (even hotter)

W

wild onion seeds – *kalongi*. Small irregular jet-black nuggets. Also known as nigella

Z

zafron – saffron

zeera – cummin

INDEX